SQL The Ultimate Beginners Guide

Learn SQl Today

Preface

This book will serve as an essential guide for you, as a SQL beginner. In addition, the concepts of SQL are laid out in a simple, concise language and instructions to help you learn the steps properly.

Specific examples and sample tables is showcased to help you practice most of the SQL queries.

Thanks again for buying this book. I hope you enjoy it!

Table of Content

Chapter 1: Definition and Purposes of SQL

For beginners, learning SQL is like learning how to speak a foreign language. You have to learn the alphabets first before you can successfully use it. Knowing the definition and purposes of SQL is crucial, before you, as a beginner can make any significant progress.

Looking at those symbols and queries may seem scary and confusing, but do not worry, the technical jargon is explained in the simplest manner to facilitate your comprehension.

What is SQL?

SQL stands for Structured Query Language. It is a standard programming language used in fetching or retrieving tables from databases. Other areas of use is creating, accessing and manipulating databases.

The most commonly used versions of the SQL are the SQL99 standard originally established by ANSI (American National Standards Institute). There is also an ORACLE version called PL/SQL, and a Microsoft version called T-SQL or Transact-SQL.

More people are growing aware of it because SQL is one of the easiest and most powerful methods of editing databases. It works in such a way that you can perform your tasks more efficiently, within a shorter timeframe.

The SQL's basis is the RDBMS (Relational Database Management System), which stores data in the form of tables.

What is a database?

A database is a collection of information, which is usually contained in electronic files stored in a computer. These files are arranged and organized so data and information can be modified and manipulated in a fast and easy way.

Purposes of SQL

There are various specific purposes of using SQL. The most common purposes are:

- Accessing Databases
- Creating and Joining Tables
- Modifying and updating tables
- Deleting Data
- Reading Data
- Retrieving and Organizing Data
- Filtering Data
- Changing and Adding Data
- Summarizing and Grouping Data

There are still various purposes of SQL that you will encounter as you read this book, so read on.

Who can use SQL?

Anyone can use SQL, as long as the person knows the commands. Database programmers, website owners and application developers, however, use SQL widely to work on their huge databases.

For a beginner, like you, you can start using basic SQL commands in organizing your files, after you have read this book.

Chapter 2: Database Basics

Databases have typical attributes that you should know. Aside from containing organized files, they have also common parts that you must get acquainted with.

These are the usual parts of an access database.

1. Tables

Tables are composed of columns and rows, with data that were usually normalized through the organization of the information. This prevents redundancies of stored data.

The columns are referred to as fields, while the rows are called records. Each of these items correspond to a different information in the database.

2. Reports

Are summaries of the data or files from the database.

They can be used to present tables of "total sales" within a month or within a year. They could also be used for printed reports or visual presentations. You can prepare formatted reports from your database of whatever summary information you may want to access.

3. Forms

Forms are the interfaces that you could use in accessing and managing your data. They are your ports of entry to your database hence they are also called data entry screens.

From your forms, you can enter commands to quickly retrieve, create, delete, add, or access a file or data.

Without your forms, it would be tedious for you to organize your databases because you have to go over your files individually.

From your forms, you can create commands that can protect your database. You can have ample control of your database such as, selecting files that only you can see, choosing files that the customer can view and protecting files that can't be viewed by the public.

On your forms, you could add other options and command buttons that you frequently use.

4. Modules

These are groups of commands and procedures that use the program, VBA (Virtual Basic for Applications), and are stored together in one unit.

There are two types of modules, the class and the standard modules. The class modules are those that is commonly attached to a specific data or file, while standard modules are found in the navigation panel.

Modules increase the functionality of your databases.

5. Queries

As previously discussed in chapter 1, there are various functions of queries (SQL) such as organizing and manipulating data. There are two types of queries, the select queries and the action queries.

The select queries have the function of selecting the data that you wish to work on, while the action queries have the function of helping you manipulate, organize, edit, add, or delete data.

All of these tasks can be displayed on your monitor or screen.

6. Macros

These are responsible in facilitating and automating your tasks when working on your databases. They provide simplified programming language that you can use to edit your databases.

They are similar to the functions of modules because they increase the functionality of your databases.

7. MySQL database server

This is one of the SQL servers or software you can use to collect and manipulate your data. You can download MySQL for free to optimize your SQL learning experience.

Similar software programs are Microsoft SQL, IBM's DB2 and Oracle SQL.

8. Operators

Operators are words or characters that are used with the WHERE clause to perform certain operations such as, number operations, logical operations, comparisons and to negate conditions. They are discussed in detail in chapter 4.

9. Predicates

Used in SQL language to identify conditions, limiting the statements.

Chapter 3: SQL Syntax and SQL Queries

SQL has its own language elements, which is executed on a CLI (Command Line Interface). These are the necessary language commands that you can utilize for your databases. This language is your SQL syntax.

On the other hand, the SQL queries are used to search the databases for the data or files that you need.

It is crucial that you understand the basic language that is used for SQL queries to proceed successfully.

The SQL syntax is the basis of SQL queries, so at times, they are interchanged with one another.

SELECT STATEMENTS and SQL Queries

These SELECT STATEMENTS are not case-sensitive, but upper case letters are used in this book to facilitate reading. So, you can use lower case letters, if you want.

SQL queries can be more specific through the use of clauses such as ORDER BY (order by), FROM (from) and WHERE (where).

- ORDER BY - is a clause that refers to the sorting of the data;

- FROM - is the designated table for the search; and

- WHERE - is the clause that defines the rows specified for the query.

Take note of the following important SQL commands too. The terms are self-explanatory but for the sake of clarity, here they are:

- SELECT – This command extracts the file/data from your database.

- CREATE DATABASE – This command creates files/data.

- DELETE – This command erases file/data from your database.

- ALTER DATABASE – This command alters the file/data in your database.

- INSERT INTO – This command will allow you to insert a new file/data into your database.

- CREATE TABLE – You can also create a new table in your database with this command.

- DROP TABLE – This command is specifically used in deleting tables in your database.

- CREATE INDEX – You can create an index with this command. An index is the search key used for your database.

- DROP INDEX – With this command, you can drop or delete your index from your

IMPORTANT REMINDERS

SQL STATEMENTS (commands) are generally separated by a semicolon. But in a few, new database systems, reportedly, they don't make use of it. So, be aware of this.

The semicolon is used to separate SQL SELECT STATEMENTS, when there are more than one statements to be executed using the same sever.

Below are examples of SELECT STATEMENTS or SQL Query

- SELECT "column_name2", "column_name3"

  FROM "table_name1"

  WHERE "column_name3"='value';

- SELECT * FROM

  WHERE "column_name"

  ORDER BY "column_name;

More keywords and SQL commands will be introduced as you read the book, so take it easy!

Chapter 4: Common Operators in SQL

As defined in chapter 2, operators are used with the WHERE clause to indicate the condition that you want performed in your tables.

You will need them to define the values in your tables.

Here are the most common operators with their corresponding symbols:

Comparison Operators

- Equal =

- Not equal <>

- Less than <

- Less than or equal <=

- Greater than >

- Greater than or equal >=

Logical operators

- **LIKE** - this keyword will allow you to retrieve the data that you will specify in your LIKE statement.

- **ALL** – this keyword is utilized to compare all values between tables.

- **BETWEEN** – this keyword displays range values within a set from the minimum to the maximum values. You can set the range of your values, using this keyword.

- **IS NULL** – this operator is used in the comparison of a value to the NULL value in a set.

- **AND** – this operator is used to add more conditions in the WHERE clause of your SQL query.

- **IN** – this compares specified values in your tables.

- **OR** – this operator is also used with the WHERE clause to specify more conditions in a SQL query.

- **ANY** – this operator compares a value to any specified value indicated in the SQL statement.

- **EXISTS** – this operator or keyword searches for the specified condition in your SQL syntax.

- **UNIQUE** – this operator will allow the display of only unique values.

Arithmetic operators

- * The asterisk, when used as an arithmetic operator, will multiple values that are found before and after the symbol.

- + The plus sign will add the values that are positioned before and after the plus sign.

- / The division sign will divide the left value with the right value of the sign.

- - The minus sign will subtract the right value from the left value.

- % The percent sign divides the left value with the right value, and displays the remainder.

Learn how to use these operators properly to optimize your SQL statements and obtain tables that can be useful to you.

Chapter 5: Commonly Used Symbols in SQL

Before you can construct or create proper and correct SQL statements or queries, you have to be familiar with the most commonly used symbols in SQL.

SQL symbols

1. Semicolon ;

This is used to end SQL statements or queries. It should always be added to complete the query. An exception is that of the Cache' SQL, which does not use semicolons.

2. Open and close parentheses ( )

These have several uses. Those are used to enclose data types, conditions and sometimes names of columns.

They are used also to enclose a subquery in the "from" clause, and arithmetic equations. In addition, when there are varied values and comma separated data.

3. Double quotes " "

These indicate delimited identifier or values.

4. Singe quotes ' '

This is used usually to enclose 'strings' of data types or conditions.

5. Asterisk *

The asterisk indicates "all" data, columns or tables.

6. Underscore _

This is used in table or column names to identify them properly. It is also used as an identifier.

7. Percent %

This is used as an identifier name for the first characters of your data such as, data names, system variables and key words.

8. Comma ,

This symbol is used as a list separator such as, in a series of columns or multiple field names.

9. Open and close square brackets [ ]

This is used to enclose a list of match data types, or characters, or pattern strings.

10.Plus +

This is usually used in number operations.

You can read more of the symbols on "conditions" in chapter 9, step #5. There are still various symbols that you can learn as your knowledge advances.

These common symbols are appropriate for a beginner, who is just starting to learn SQL.

Chapter 6: How to Create Databases

As a beginner in SQL, you must know how to create DATABASES. Databases are simply systematic collections of data that can be stored in your computer, where they can be retrieved easily for future use.

The system is called DBMS (Database Management System), and is used extensively by all institutions that need to store large volumes of information or data.

Examples of data are: Name, Age, Address, Country, ID number and all vital information that have to be organized and stored.

The retrieval of these databases is possible through database software or programs such as, SQL, MySQL, ORACLE and other similar apps.

Creating databases is simple with this SQL statement:

Example: CREATE DATABASE "database_name";

If you want to create a "MyStudents" database, you can state the SQL query this way:

Example: CREATE DATABASE MyStudents;

If you want to create a "My_Sales" database, you can state your SQL this way:

Example: CREATE DATABASE My_Sales;

The names of your databases must be unique within the RDBMS (Relational Database Management System). After creating your database, you can now create tables for your databases.

You can double check if your database exists by this SQL query:

Example: SHOW DATABASES;

This SQL statement will display all the databases that you have created.

It is important to note that your ability to retrieve or fetch the data that you have stored is one vital consideration.

Therefore, you have to choose the most applicable and most appropriate SQL server or software that you can optimize and synchronize with the computer you are using.

Chapter 7: Data Types

There are various data types that you should be familiar with. This is because they make use of SQL language that are significant in understanding SQL more.

There are six SQL data types

1. Date and Time Data

As the name implies, this type of data deals with date and time.

Examples are: datetime (FROM Feb 1, 1816 TO July 2, 8796), smalldatetime (FROM Feb 1, 2012 TO Mar 2085, date (Jun 1, 2016) and time (3:20 AM.).

2. Exact Numeric Data

Under exact numeric data, there are several subtypes too such as;

- *tinyint* – FROM 0 TO 255

- *bit* – FROM 0 TO 1

- bigint – FROM -9,223,372,036,854,775,808 TO 9,223,372,036,854,775,807

- *numeric* – FROM $-10^{38}+1$ TO $10^{38}-1$

- *int* - FROM -2,147,483,648 TO 2,147,483,647

- *decimal* – FROM $-10^{38}+1$ TO $10^{38}-1$

- *money* – FROM -922,337,203,685,477.5808 TO 922,337,203,685,477.5807

- *smallmoney* – FROM -214,748.3648 TO +214,748.3647

- *smallint* – FROM -32,768 TO 32,767

3. Binary Data

Binary data have different types, as well. These are: Binary (fixed), varbinary (variable length binary) varbinary (max) (variable length binary) and image.

They are classified according to the length of their bytes, with Binary having the shortest and the fixed value.

4. Approximate Numeric Data

These have two types, the float and the real. The float has a value FROM - 1.79E +308 TO 1.79E +308, while the real data has a value FROM -3.40E +38 TO 3.40E +38

5. Unicode Character Strings Data

There are four types of Unicode Character Strings Data namely; ntext, nchar, nvarchar, and nvarchar (max). They are classified according to their character lengths.

For ntext, it has a maximum character length of 1,073,741,823, which is variable.

For nchar, it has a unicode maximum fixed length of 4,000 characters.

For nvarchar (max), it has a unicode variable maximum length of 231 characters.

For nvarchar, it has a variable maximum length of 4,000 unicode characters.

6. Character Strings Data

The character Strings Data have almost similar types as the Unicode Character Strings Data, only, some have different maximum values and they are non-unicode characters, as well.

For text, it has a maximum variable length of 2,147,483,647 non-unicode characters.

For char, it has a non-unicode maximum fixed length of 8,000 characters.

For varchar (max), it has a non-unicode variable maximum length of 231 characters.

For varchar, it has a variable maximum length of 8,000 non-unicode characters.

Miscellaneous Data

Aside from the 6 major types of data, miscellaneous data are also stored as tables, SQL variants, cursors, XML files, unique identifiers, cursors and/or timestamps.

You can refer to this chapter when you want to know about the maximum values of the data you are preparing.

It helps to have some information on these values.

Chapter 8: Downloading SQL Software

Although, almost all of the SQL queries presented here are general, it would be easy for you to adjust to whatever type of SQL server you will be using, eventually.

Before you can perform any SQL task in your computer, you have first to download a SQL software.

There are various choices you can select from. But since you're a beginner, you can use the free MySQL databases software. Hence, we will be focusing on how to download this application.

What is MySQL?

MySQL is a tool (database server) that uses SQL syntax to manage databases. It is an RDBMS (Relational Database Management System) that you can use to facilitate the manipulation of your databases.

If you are managing a website using MySQL, ascertain that the host of your website supports MySQL too.

Here's how you can install MySQL in your Microsoft Windows. We will be using Windows because it is the most common application used in computers.

How to install MySQL on Microsoft Windows in your computer.

Step #1 – Go to the MySQL website

Go to www.mysql.com and browse through the applications to select MySQL. Ascertain that you obtain the MySQL from its genuine website to prevent downloading viruses, which can be harmful to your computer.

Step #2 – Select the 'download' option

Next, click on the download option this will bring you to the MySQL Community Server, and to the MySQL Community Edition. Click 'download'.

Step #3 – Choose your Windows' processor version

Choose your Windows' processor version by perusing the details given on the page. Choose from the 'other downloads' label. You can choose either the 32-bit or 64-bit.

27

Click the download button for the Windows (x86, 32-bit), ZIP Archive or the Windows (x86, 64-bit), ZIP Archive, whichever is applicable to your computer.

Step #4 – Register on the site

Before you can download your selected version, you will be requested to register by answering the sign in form for an Oracle account.

You don't have to reply to the questions that are optional. You can also click on the 'no thanks' button.

There is another option of just downloading the server without signing up, but you will not be enjoying some freebies such as, being able to download some white papers and technical information, faster access to MySQL downloads and other services.

Step #5 – Sign in to your MySQL account

After registering, you can sign in now to your new account. A new page will appear, where you can select your area through the displayed images of flags. Afterwards, you can click the download button and save it in your computer.

This can take several minutes.

Step #6 – Name the downloaded file

After downloading the file. You can name your MySQL file and save it in your desktop or C drive. It's up to you, whichever you prefer.

Step #7 – Install your MySQL Server

Click the file to open it and then click 'install' to install MySQL in your computer. This will open a small window in which your computer will ask if you want to open and install the program. Just click the "OK" button.

Step #8 – Browse your MySQL packages

The MySQL Enterprise Server page will appear giving you some information about what your MySQL package contains.

There are packages offered for a small fee, but since we're just interested in the community server, just click 'next' until you reached the 'finish' button.

Step #9 – Uncheck the box 'Register the MySQL Server now'

After the Wizard has completed the set-up, a box appears asking you to configure and register your MySQL Server. Uncheck the 'Register the MySQL Server now' box, and check the small box for the "Configure the MySQL Server now'.

Then click 'finish'.

Step #10 – Click 'next' on the Configuration Wizard box

A box will appear, and you just have to click next.

Step #11 – Select the configuration type

A box will appear asking you to select your configuration type. Tick the small circle for the 'Detailed Configuration', instead of the 'Standard Configuration'. Click the 'next' button.

Step #12 – Select the server type

There will be three choices; the Developer Machine, the Server Machine and the Dedicated MySQL Server Machine.

Select the Server Machine because it will have medium memory usage, which is ideal for a beginner like you, who is interested to learn more about MySQL.

The Developer Machine uses minimal memory and may not allow you the maximize usage of your MySQL.

On the other hand, the MySQL Server Machine is for people who work as database programmers or full time MySQL users. It will use all of the available memory in your computer, so it is not recommended for you.

Step #13 – Select the database usage

For database usage, there are three choices, namely; Multifunctional Database, Transactional Database Only, and Non-Transactional Database Only. Choose the Multifunctional Database because your purpose is for general purposes.

The Transactional and Non-transactional are used for more specific purposes.

Click the 'next' button at the bottom of the display box.

Step #14 – Select the drive for the InnoDB datafile

If you do not want to use the 'default' settings, you can select the drive from your computer, where you want to store your InnoDB datafile. Choose the drive you prefer and then click 'next'.

Step #15 - Set the number of concurrent connections to the server

This will indicate the number of users that will be connecting simultaneously to your server. The choices are; Discussion

Support (DSS)/OLAP, Online Transaction Processing (OLTP) and Manual Setting.

It is recommended that you choose the option, DSS/OLAP because you will not be requiring a high number of concurrent connection. OLTP is needed for highly loaded servers, while the manual setting can be bothersome to be setting it every now and then.

After setting this, click 'next'.

Step #16 – Set the networking options

Enable the TCP/IP Networking by checking the small box before it. Below it, add your port number and then check the small box for Enable Strict Mode to set the server SQL mode.

Click 'next'.

Step #17 – Select the default character set

The most recommended is the Standard Character Set because it is suited for English and other West European languages. It is also the default for English.

The other two choices namely; Best Support For Multilingualism and the Manual Default Character Set are best for those who have other languages other than English.

Tick the small circle before the Standard Character Set and click 'next'.

Step #18 – Set the Windows options

Tick the two choices displayed, which are; Install As Windows Server and Include Bin Directory in Windows Path. This will allow you to work with your MySQL from your command line.

Selecting the Install As Windows Server will automatically display the Service Name. The small box below the Service Name must be checked too.

Click 'next'.

Step #19 – Set the security options

Set your password. The box will indicate where you can type it.

Click 'next'.

Step #20 - Execute your configurations

All you have to do is to click 'execute' and your computer will configure by itself based on your specifications.

Once configuration is complete and all the boxes are checked, click 'finish'.

Step #21 – Set verification process

- Go to the start menu and type cmd and press enter. This will take you to the command panel.

- Type the following:

  mysql -u root -p

Press 'enter'.

Take note that there is a space between mysql and the dash symbol, and between u and root. Also, there is a space between root and the dash symbol.

- The command panel will ask for your password. Type your password and press 'enter'.

- A mysql prompt will appear.

- You can type any SQL command to display the databases. Remember to add the semicolon at the end of your SQL statement.

- Close your command panel for the meantime.

Using your MySQL can motivate you to learn more about other related applications such as, PHP, and similar products.

What is important is for you to learn the basics of SQL first.

Chapter 9: How to Create Tables

Your tables are used to store the data or information in your database. They are composed of rows and columns as discussed in chapter 1. Specific names are assigned to the tables to identify them properly and to facilitate their manipulation. The rows of the tables contain the information for the columns.

Knowing how to create tables is important for a beginner, who wants to learn SQL.

The following are the simple steps:

Step #1 – Enter the keywords CREATE TABLE

These keywords will express your intention and direct what action you have in mind.

Example: CREATE TABLE

Step #2 – Enter the table name

Right after your CREATE TABLE keywords, add the table name. The table name should be specific and unique to allow easy and quick access later on.

Example: CREATE TABLE "table_name"

The name of your table must not be easy to guess by anyone. You can do this by including your initials and your birthdate.

If your name is Henry Sheldon, and your birthdate is October 20, 1964, you can add that information to the name of your table.

Let's say you want your table to be about the traffic sources in your website, you can name the table "traffic_hs2064"

Take note that all SQL statements must end with a semicolon (;). All the data variables must be enclosed with quotation marks (" "), as well.

> Example: CREATE TABLE traffic_hs2064

Step #3 – Add an open parenthesis in the next line

The parenthesis will indicate the introduction of the columns you want to create.

> Example: CREATE TABLE "table_name"
>
> (

Let's apply this step to our specific example.

> Example: CREATE TABLE traffic_hs2064
>
> (

In some instances, the parentheses are not used.

Step #4 – Add the first column name

What do you want to name your first column? This should be related to the data or information you want to collect for your table. Always separate your column definitions with a comma.

Example: CREATE TABLE "table_name"

("column_name" "data type",

In our example, the focus of the table is on the traffic sources of your website. Hence, you can name the first column "country".

Example: CREATE TABLE traffic_hs2064

(country

Step #4 – Add more columns based on your data

You can add more columns if you need more data about your table. It's up to you. So, if you want to add four more columns, this is how your SQL statement would appear.

Example: CREATE TABLE "table_name"

("column_name1" "data type",

"column_name2" "data type",

"column_name3" "data type",

"column_name4" "data type");

Don't forget to add the closing parenthesis and the semi-colon after the SQL statement.

Let's say you have decided to add for column 2 the keyword used in searching for your website, for column 3, the number of minutes that the visitor had spent on your website, and for column 4, the particular post that the person visited. This is how your SQL statement would appear.

Take note:

- The name of the table or column must start with a letter, then it can be followed by a number, an underscore, or another letter. It's preferable that the number of the characters does not exceed 30.

- You can also use a VARCHAR (variable-length character) data type to help create the column.

- **Common data types are:**
  - **date** – date specified or value
  - **number (size)** – you should specify the maximum number of column digits inside the open and close parentheses
  - **char (size)** – you should specify the size of the fixed length inside the open and close parentheses.
  - **varchar (size)** – you should specify the maximum size inside the open and close parentheses. This is for variable lengths of the entries.
  - **Number (size, d)** – This is similar to number (size), except that 'd' represents the maximum number of digits (from the decimal point) to the right of the number.

Hence if you want your column to show 10.21, your date type would be:

number (2,2)

Example: CREATE TABLE traffic_hs2064

(country varchar (40),

keywords varchar (30),

time number (3),

post varchar (40));

Step #5 – Add CONSTRAINTS, if any

CONSTRAINTS are rules that are applied for a particular column. You can add CONSTRAINTS, if you wish. The most common CONSTRAINTS are:

- o **"NOT NULL"** – this indicates that the columns should not contain blanks

- o **"UNIQUE"** – this indicates that all entries added must be unique and not similar to any item on that particular column.

In summary, creating a table using a SQL statement will start with the CREATE TABLE, then the "table name", then an open parenthesis, then the "column names", the "data type", (add a comma after every column), then add any "CONSTRAINTS".

Don't forget to add the closing parenthesis and the semicolon at the end of your SQL statement.

Chapter 10: Deleting Tables

Deleting tables, rows or columns from your database is easy by using appropriate SQL statements. This is one of the commands that you must know to be able to optimize your introductory lessons to SQL.

Here are steps in deleting tables:

Step #1 – Select the DELETE command

On your monitor, choose the DELETE command and press the key. Downloading Window's MySQL Database, MySQL Connectors and MySQL Workbench can facilitate your process.

Expert SQL users may laugh and say that these steps should not be included in this book. But for beginners, it is crucial to state specifically what steps should be done. Imagine yourself learning a totally new language; Russian for example, and you'll know what I mean.

Step #2 – Indicate from what table

You can do this by adding the word "FROM" and the name of the table

        DELETE FROM 'table_name"

Make sure you have selected the proper table_name. Using our first sample example from the previous chapter, this is how your SQL statement would appear:

Example: DELETE from traffic_hs2064

Step #3 – Indicate the specific column or row by adding "where"

If you don't indicate the "where" all your files would be deleted, so ensure that your statement is complete.

Example: DELETE FROM 'table_name"

WHERE "column_name"

Hence, if you want to delete the entire table, simply choose:

DELETE FROM "table_name";

Using our previous example from chapter 1, this is how your SQL statement would appear:

Example: DELETE FROM traffic_hs2064

where time = (10)

DELETE from traffic_hs2064

where time = (5);

Step #4 – Complete your DELETE statement by adding the necessary variables

Example: DELETE FROM "table_name"

WHERE "column_name"

OPERATOR "value"

[AND/OR "column"

OPERATOR "value"];

Deleting the wrong tables from your database can cause problems, so, ascertain that you have entered the correct SQL statements.

Chapter 11: Inserting Data into a Table

You can insert a new data into an existing table through the following steps.

Step #1 – Enter the key words INSERT INTO

Select the key words INSERT INTO. The most common program, which is compatible with SQL is windows MySQL. You can use this to insert data into your table.

Step #2 - Add the table name

Next, you can now add the table name. Be sure it is the correct table

Example: INSERT INTO "table_name"

Using our own table:

Example: INSERT INTO traffic_hs2064

Step #3 – Add Open parenthesis

You can now add your open parenthesis after the table name and before the column_names. Remember to add commas after each column.

Example: INSERT INTO "table_name"

(

Using our own table:

Example: INSERT INTO traffic_hs2064

(

Step #4 – Indicate the column

Indicate the column where you intend to insert your data.

Example: INSERT INTO "table_name"

("column _name", . . . "column_name"

Step #5 – Close the columns with a close parenthesis

Don't forget to add your closing parenthesis. This will indicate that you have identified the columns accordingly.

Example: INSERT INTO "table_name"

("first_columnname",   .   .   .
"last_columnname")

Step #6 – Add the key word values

The key word values will help your selection be more specific. This is followed by the list of values. These values must be enclosed in parentheses too.

Example: INSERT INTO "table_name"

("first_columnname",   .   .   .
"last_columnname")

values (first_value, . . . last_value

Step #7 – Add the closing parenthesis

Remember to add the close parenthesis to your SQL statement. This will indicate that the column does not go no further.

Example: INSERT INTO "table_name"

("first_columnname",   .   .   .
"last_columnname")

values (first_value, . . . last_value)

Step #8 – Add your semicolon

All SQL statements end up with a semicolon, with the exception of a few.

Example: INSERT INTO "table_name"

("first_columnname",   .   .   .
"last_columnname")

values (first_value, . . . last_value);

Take note that strings must be enclosed in single quotation marks, while numbers are not.

Using our sample table, you can come up with this SQL statement:

Example: INSERT INTO "traffic_hs2064"

(country, keyword. time)

values ('America', 'marketing', 10);

You can insert more data safely without affecting the other tables. Just make sure you're using the correct SQL commands or statements.

Chapter 12: Dropping a Table

You can drop or delete a table with a few strokes on your keyboard. But before you decide to drop or delete a table, think about the extra time you may spend restoring it back, if you happen to need it later on. So, be careful with this command.

Dropping a table

Dropping a table is different from deleting the records/data in the table. When you drop a table, you are deleting the table definition plus the records/data in the table.

>Example: DROP TABLE "table_name"

Using our table, the SQL statement would read like this.

>Example: DROP TABLE traffic_hs2064;

Deleting data in a table

As discussed in the earlier chapters, this action will delete all the records/data in your table but will not delete the table itself. Hence, if your table structure is not deleted, you can insert data later on.

The complete steps in deleting data or record in a table are discussed in another chapter.

DROPPING your table is easy as long as you are able to create the proper SQL.

Chapter 13: Selecting Data

Selecting a datum from your database can be done through the SELECT key. You only have to specify the data you want to select.

Step #1 – Choose the SELECT statement

Choose SELECT to identify your SQL command.

Step #2 – Choose the column

Choose the specific column where you want to retrieve the data.

> Example: SELECT "column_name"

Step #3 – Use the asterisk * to select all columns

If you want to select all columns use *, or you can also choose as many columns as you want.

> Example: SELECT "column_name1"
>
> ["column_name2", "column_name3"]

Step #4 – Add FROM and the table name, where the data will come from

You can enclose the identified columns and where conditions with open and close square brackets [ ], but this is optional.

Example: SELECT "column_name"

["column_name", "column_name"]

FROM 'table_name"

WHERE "colum_name";

You can also write the above example in this way:

Example: select   column_name,   column_name, column_name

from table_name

where column_name;

Step #5 – Specify the "CONDITION"

You can specify the condition through the common operators that are presented in chapter 4.

Example #1: SELECT "column_name"

["column_name", "column_name"]

FROM 'table_name"

[where "colum_name" "condition"];

You can also write the above example in this way: (no open and close square brackets)

Example #2: select column_name, column_name, column_name

from table_name

where column_name condition;

Example #3: SELECT "column_name"

[, "column_name", "column_name"]

FROM "table_name"

[WHERE "column_name" LIKE 'Am'];

In the example above, all entries that start or match with 'Am' will be displayed.

Example: SELECT "column_name"

FROM "table_name"

WHERE "column_name" = 'America';

In the example above, only the rows that exactly matches or equals 'America' will be selected.

Reminder:

You can remove the double quotes when using the actual names of the tables and columns.

Chapter 14: Sample SQL Queries

Before we proceed further, let's have some exercises for the simple SQL queries. A sample table is presented below to serve as your practice table.

Sample table Traffic_hs2064

Traffic_hs2064

Country	Searchword	Time (minutes)	Post
America	perfect	5	Matchmaker
Italy	partner	2	NatureTripping
Sweden	mate	10	Fiction
Spain	couple	3	News
Malaysia	team	6	Health
Philippines	island	5	Entertainment
Africa	lover	4	Opinion

From the table above, construct or create your SQL statements, syntax or queries from the following instances.

1. Retrieve country, time and post only.

2. Retrieve country, searchword and post.

3. Retrieve all columns for every country that shows a time that is less than 5 minutes.

4. Retrieve all columns for every country that shows a time of more than 6 minutes.

5. Retrieve all columns for every country that contains 'America'.

6. Retrieve all files.

7. Retrieve all columns for every country that is not 'America'.

8. Retrieve searchword and post only.

9. Retrieve country and post only.

10. Retrieve all columns for every country, which name equals 'Italy'.

Try answering the exercises listed above on your computer, before looking at the answers. You can also use a pencil and paper, so you can tweak your answers, if you feel more comfortable with this method.

Remember that your SQL command or key words (SELECT, DELETE, DROP TABLE, and similar statements) are not case sensitive, so you can use either the lower case or upper case.

The column names and table names are not case sensitive in Microsoft but with UNIX, table names are case sensitive. You have to take note of the database software you are using.

When you retrieve the data, the results of your SQL query should, supposedly, be displayed on your monitor.

Here are answers; the SQL statements and the resulting tables (outputs)

1. SQL statement:

SELECT country, time, post FROM traffic_hs2064;

Resulting table

Traffic_hs2064

Country	Time (minutes)	Post
America	5	Matchmaker
Italy	2	NatureTripping
Sweden	10	Fiction
Spain	3	News
Malaysia	6	Health
Philippines	5	Entertainment
Africa	4	Opinion

2. SQL statement:

SELECT country, searchword, post FROM traffic_hs2064;

Resulting table

Traffic_hs2064

Country	Searchword	Post

America	perfect	Matchmaker
Italy	partner	NatureTripping
Sweden	mate	Fiction
Spain	couple	News
Malaysia	team	Health
Philippines	island	Entertainment
Africa	lover	Opinion

3. SQL statement:

SELECT country, searchword, time, post FROM traffic_hs2064

where time < 5;

or you could also state it this way:

SELECT * from traffic_hs2064 where time < 5;

Resulting table

Traffic_hs2064

Country	Searchword	Time (minutes)	Post
Italy	partner	2	NatureTripping
Spain	couple	3	News
Africa	lover	4	Opinion

4. SQL statement:

SELECT country, searchword, time, post FROM traffic_hs2064

WHERE time > 6;

or you could also express it this way:

SELECT * FROM traffic_hs2064 WHERE time > 6;

Resulting table

Traffic_hs2064

Country	Searchword	Time (minutes)	Post
Sweden	mate	10	Fiction

5. SQL statement:

SELECT * FROM traffic_hs2064

WHERE country = 'America';

Resulting table

Traffic_hs2064

Country	Searchword	Time (minutes)	Post

| America | perfect | 5 | Matchmaker |

6. SQL statement:

SELECT * FROM traffic_hs2064

Resulting table

Traffic_hs2064

Country	Searchword	Time (minutes)	Post
America	perfect	5	Matchmaker
Italy	partner	2	NatureTripping
Sweden	mate	10	Fiction
Spain	couple	3	News
Malaysia	team	6	Health
Philippines	island	5	Entertainment
Africa	lover	4	Opinion

7. SQL statement:

SELECT * FROM traffic_hs2064 WHERE country < > 'America';

Resulting table

Traffic_hs2064

Country	Searchword	Time (minutes)	Post
Italy	partner	2	NatureTripping
Sweden	mate	10	Fiction
Spain	couple	3	News
Malaysia	team	6	Health
Philippines	island	5	Entertainment
Africa	lover	4	Opinion

8. SQL statement:

SELECT searchword, post FROM traffic_hs2064;

Traffic_hs2064

Searchword	Post
perfect	Matchmaker
partner	NatureTripping
mate	Fiction
couple	News
team	Health
island	Entertainment

lover	Opinion

9. SQL statement:

SELECT country, post FROM traffic_hs2064;

Resulting table

Traffic_hs2064

Country	Post
America	Matchmaker
Italy	NatureTripping
Sweden	Fiction
Spain	News
Malaysia	Health
Philippines	Entertainment
Africa	Opinion

10. SQL statement:

SELECT * FROM traffic_hs2064 WHERE country = 'Italy';

Resulting table

Traffic_hs2064

Country	Searchword	Time (minutes)	Post
Italy	partner	2	NatureTripping

These are basic SQL statements or queries that you must know before you can proceed to more complex forms.

Practice more with your own SQL software. Of course, by now, you should have downloaded an SQL program in your computer. Windows' MySQL program and Microsoft SQL server are more preferable for beginners.

Chapter 15: Combining and Joining Tables

There will be times that you have to combine tables. This task can be more complex than simply creating tables. But like everything that you do, the difficulty is all in your mind. If you think you can, then you can. So, here goes.

The steps in combining tables are the following:

Step #1 – SELECT the columns you want to combine

You can indicate this with the SQL key word SELECT. This will display the columns you want to combine.

Example: SELECT "column_name", "colum_name"

FROM "table_name"

Step #2 – Add the keyword UNION

Add the key word UNION to indicate your intent of combining the tables.

Example: SELECT "column_name", "column_name"

from "table_name"

UNION

Step #3 – SELECT the other columns

Now, SELECT the other columns you want to combine with your first selected columns.

Example: SELECT "column_name", "column_name" FROM "table_name"

UNION   SELECT   "column_name", "column_name" FROM "table_name";

Step #4 – Use UNION ALL, in some cases

You can proceed to this step, in cases, when you want to include duplicate data. Without the key word "ALL", duplicate data would automatically be deleted.

Example: SELECT "column_name", "column_name" FROM "table_name"

UNION   ALL   SELECT   "column_name", "column_name" FROM "table_name";

Combining tables with the SQL statement SELECT and JOIN

When your database server cannot handle the heavy load of your SELECT UNION query, you could also use the keyword JOIN.

The same steps apply for these statements. All you have to do is add the appropriate JOIN keyword.

There are many types of JOIN SQL queries. These are:

- **INNER JOIN (SIMPLE JOIN)** – This will return or retrieve all data from tables that are joined. However, columns will not be displayed when one of the joined tables has no data.

Example: SELECT "column1", "column2" FROM "table_name1"

INNER JOIN "table_name2"

ON "table_name1".column" = "table_name2.column";

Let's say you have the following two tables:

Table A

Students

Student No	LastName	FirstName	Age	Address	City
1	Potter	Michael	17	130 Reed Ave.	Cheyenne
2	Walker	Jean	18	110 Westlake	Cody
3	Anderson	Ted	18	22 Staten Sq.	Laramie

| 4 | Dixon | Allan | 18 | 12 Glenn Rd. | Casper |
| 5 | Cruise | Timothy | 19 | 20 Reed Ave. | Cheyenne |

Table B

StudentInformation

StudentNo	Year	Average
1	1st	90
2	1st	87
3	3rd	88
4	5th	77
5	2nd	93

You may want to extract specified data from both tables. Let's say from table A, you want to display LastName, FirstName and the City, while from Table B, you want to display the Average.

You can construct your SQL statement this way:

Example:

SELECT Students.LastName, Students.FirstName, StudentInformation.Average

FROM Students

INNER JOIN StudentInformation ON Students.StudentNo= StudentInformation.StudentNo;

This SQL query will display these data on your resulting table:

LastName	FirstName	Average
Potter	Michael	90
Walker	Jean	87
Anderson	Ted	88
Dixon	Allan	77
Cruise	Timothy	93

- **LEFT OUTER JOIN (LEFT JOIN)** – This SQL statement will display all rows from the left hand table (table 1), even if these do not match with the right hand table (table 2).

  With the ON key word, it will display only the rows specified. Data from the other table will only be displayed, if the data intersect with the first selected table.

Example: SELECT "column1", "column2" from "table_name1"

LEFT (OUTER) JOIN "table_name2"

ON   "table_name1".column"   =
"table_name2.column";

Let's use the two base tables above and create LEFT JOIN with the tables to display the LastName and the Year. You can create your SQL statement this way:

Example: SELECT   students.LastName, StudentInformation.Year

FROM students

LEFT JOIN StudentInformation

ON   Students.StudentNo   =
StudentInformation.StudentNo;

Your resulting table will appear this way:

LastName	Year
Potter	1st
Walker	1st
Anderson	3rd
Dixon	5th

Cruise	2nd

- **RIGHT OUTER JOIN (RIGHT JOIN)** – This query will display all the rows from the right hand table (table 2). With the ON key word added, just like with the LEFT JOIN, it will display only the rows specified.

This SQL statement will display all data from table 2, even if there are no matches from table 1 (left table). Take note that only the data from table 1 that intersect with table 2 will be displayed.

Example: SELECT "column1", "column2" from "table_name1"

RIGHT (OUTER) JOIN "table_name2"

ON   "table_name1".column"   = "table_name2.column";

Let's use the same base tables above, to facilitate viewing, the two base tables are shown again on this page.

Table A

Students

Student No	LastNa me	FirstNa me	Ag e	Addres s	City

1	Potter	Michael	17	130 Reed Ave.	Cheyenne
2	Walker	Jean	18	110 Westlake	Cody
3	Anderson	Ted	18	22 Staten Sq.	Laramie
4	Dixon	Allan	18	12 Glenn Rd.	Casper
5	Cruise	Timothy	19	20 Reed Ave.	Cheyenne

Table B

StudentInformation

StudentNo	Year	Average
1	1st	90
2	1st	87
3	3rd	88
4	5th	77
5	2nd	93

And you want to perform a RIGHT OUTER JOIN or a RIGHT JOIN.

Here's how you can state your SQL query.

Example: SELECT   Students.City, StudentInformation.Average

FROM Students

RIGHT JOIN StudentInformation

ON   students.StudentNo   = StudentInformation.StudentNo

ORDER BY Students.City;

Your result-table will appear like this:

City	Average
Cheyenne	90
Casper	77
Cheyenne	93
Cody	87
Laramie	88

- **FULL OUTER JOIN (FULL JOIN)** – This SQL keyword will display all the rows from both the left and right hand tables.

  All data should be displayed by a query using these keywords. Take note that you should insert nulls when the conditions are not met in the joined tables

Example: SELECT "column1", "column2" from "table_name1"

FULL (OUTER) JOIN "table_name2"

ON   "table_name1"."column"   = "table_name2"."column";

Using the two base tables above, you can create your SQL FULL JOIN statement this way:

Example: SELECT   Students.LastName, StudentInformation.Average

FROM Students

FULL JOIN StudentInformation

ON   students.StudentNo   = StudentInformation.StudentNo

ORDER BY Students.LastName;

This will be your table output:

LastName	Average
Potter	90
Anderson	93
Cruise	88
Dixon	87
Walker	77

There are no NULL VALUES in any of the columns because the column in both tables matched.

- **CROSS JOIN** – This SQL key word will display each row from table1 that combined with each row from table2.

  This is also called the CARTESIAN JOIN.

  Example: SELECT * from ["table_name1"] CROSS JOIN ["table_name2"];

Using the two base tables above, we can create a SQL statement this way:

Example: SELECT * from Students CROSS JOIN StudentInformation;

The output-table will be this:

Studen tNo	LastNa me	FirstNa me	Ag e	Addre ss	City	Ye ar	Avera ge

1	Potter	Michael	17	130 Reed Ave.	Cheyenne	1st	90
2	Walker	Jean	18	110 Westlake	Cody	1st	87
3	Anderson	Ted	18	22 Staten Sq.	Laramie	3rd	88
4	Dixon	Allan	18	12 Glenn Rd.	Casper	5th	77
5	Cruise	Timothy	19	20 Reed Ave.	Cheyenne	2nd	93

Making use of this JOIN SQL syntax properly can save time and money. Use them to your advantage.

Take note that when the WHERE clause is used, the CROSS JOIN becomes an INNER JOIN.

There is also one way of expressing your CROSS JOIN. The SQL can be created this way:

Example: SELECT LastName, FirstName, Age, Address, City

FROM Students

CROSS JOIN StudentInformation;

There will be slight variations in the SQL statements of other SQL servers, but the main syntax is typically basic.

Chapter 16: Pivoting Data

Pivoting data is converting your data, which are presented in rows, into column presentations.

Through the use of PIVOT queries, you can manipulate the rows and columns to present variations of the table that will help you in analyzing your table. PIVOT can present a column into multiple columns. You have also the option to use UNPIVOT query. UNPIVOT does the opposite of what PIVOT does.

It is extremely useful in multidimensional reporting. You may need it in generating your numerous reports.

How can you compose your PIVOT query?

Step #1 – Ascertain that your SQL can allow PIVOT queries

Is the version of your SQL server appropriate for PIVOT queries. If not, then you cannot accomplish these specific queries.

Step #2 - Determine what you want displayed in your results

Identify the column or data you want to appear in your results or output page.

Step #3 – Prepare your PIVOT query, using SQL

Use your knowledge of SQL to compose or create your PIVOT query.

To understand more about PIVOT, let's use the table below as a base table.

ProductSales

ProductName	Year	Earnings
RazorBlades1	2015	12000.00
BarHandles1	2016	15000.00
RazorBlades2	2015	10000.00
BarHandles2	2016	11000.00

Let's say you want an output that will show the ProductName as the column headings. This would be your PIVOT query:

Example #1:

SELECT * FROM ProductSales

PIVOT (SUM(Earnings)

FOR ProductNames IN ([RazorBlades1], [BarHandles1], [RazorBlades2], [BarHandles2]) AS PVT

With the PIVOT query above, your ProductSales table will now appear like this:

#ProductNamesPIVOTResults

ProductName	RazorBlades1	BarHandles1	RazorBlades2	BarHandles2
Year	2015	2016	2015	2016
Earnings	12000.00	15000.00	10000.00	11000.00

You can also manipulate the table based on your preferences.

Example #2

If you want the Year to be the column headings, you can write your PIVOT query this way:

SELECT * FROM ProductSales

PIVOT (SUM(EARNINGS)

FOR Year IN ([2015], [2016]) AS PVT

The resulting output would be the table below:

YearPivotResult

ProductName	2015	2016
RazorBlades1	12000.00	NULL
BarHandles1	15000.00	NULL
RazorBlades2	NULL	10000.00
BarHandles2	NULL	11000.00

There are more ways for you to use your PIVOT query.

For your UNPIVOT query, it will work the opposite way your PIVOT query does. It will convert the columns into rows.

Example

Using Exercise #1, you can come up with this UNPIVOT query:

SELECT ProductName, Year, Earnings

FROM #ProductNamesPivotResult

UNPIVOT (Earnings FOR ProductName IN ([RazorBlades1], [BarHandles1], [RazorBlades2], [BarHandles2]) AS UPVT

The output would be the original table:

#ProductSalesUnpivotResult

ProductName	Year	Earnings
RazorBlades1	2015	12000.00
BarHandles1	2016	15000.00
RazorBlades2	2015	10000.00
BarHandles2	2016	11000.00

Chapter 17: Updating Data

Updating or changing data is one task you must learn and engage in as a beginner SQL learner.

The key word for this SQL query is UPDATE. You can follow the steps below.

Step #1 – Create your UPDATE syntax

Prepare your update SQL query or syntax by using the key word UPDATE.

Example: UPDATE "table_name"

SET   "column_name1"   =   value1, "column_name2"= value2;

Step #2 – Add the WHERE clause

Be sure to include the WHERE clause to identify the columns to be updated, otherwise, all of your data will be updated.

Example: UPDATE "table_name"

SET   "column_name1"   =   value1, "column_name2"= value2

WHERE   some   _"column_name"=
some_value;

Step #3 – Double check your SQL syntax

You must double check your statement before clicking the enter button. One error can cause problems in your database.

Let's practice making UPDATE SQL statements from the table below. The table below is on "Online Students".

Students

StudentNo	LastName	FirstName	Age	Address	City
1	Potter	Michael	17	130 Reed Ave.	Cheyenne
2	Walker	Jean	18	110 Westlake	Cody
3	Anderson	Ted	18	22 Staten Sq.	Laramie
4	Dixon	Allan	18	12 Glenn	Casper

				Rd.	
5	Cruise	Timothy	19	20 Reed Ave.	Cheyenne
6	Depp	Adam	17	276 Grand Ave.	Laramie
7	Lambert	David	19	32 8th St.	Cody
8	Cowell	Janine	18	140 Center St.	Casper
9	Kennedy	Daniel	17	11 21st St.	Laramie
10	Budzinak	Leila	20	24 Wing St.	Cheyenne

EXERCISE #1

Let's say you want to update or change the student "Walker, Jean" with a new address and city. How would you state your SQL query?

ANSWER:

Your SQL statement should appear this way:

Example: UPDATE students

SET Address = '34 Staten Sq', City = 'Laramie'

WHERE LastName = 'Walker';

REMINDER: AGAIN, Always indicate the WHERE clause to prevent updating all the data in your table.

If you have submitted the correct SQL query, your resulting table will appear like this:

Students

StudentNo	LastName	FirstName	Age	Address	City
1	Potter	Michael	17	130 Reed Ave.	Cheyenne
2	Walker	Jean	18	34 Staten Sq.	Laramie
3	Anderson	Ted	18	22 Staten Sq.	Laramie
4	Dixon	Allan	18	12 Glenn Rd.	Casper
5	Cruise	Timothy	19	20 Reed	Cheyenne

				Ave.	
6	Depp	Adam	17	276 Grand Ave.	Laramie
7	Lambert	David	19	32 8th St.	Cody
8	Cowell	Janine	18	140 Center St.	Casper
9	Kennedy	Daniel	17	11 21st St.	Laramie
10	Budzinak	Leila	20	24 Wing St.	Cheyenne

EXERCISE #2

You want to update the address of Cowell, Janine to 20 18th St. Laramie City. What would your SQL syntax be?

Try creating your SQL statement without looking at the answer.

ANSWER:

UPDATE students

SET Address = '2018th St.', City = 'Laramie'

WHERE LastName = 'Budzinak';

If your SQL query is correct, your table will be updated according to your recent input.

Chapter 18: Filtering Data

Filtering data is an essential skill that you can learn as a beginner. There are various filtering activities that have been previously discussed in the past chapters by the use of the SQL keyword WHERE.

Filtering the data is similar to selecting the data you want to be displayed on your monitors.

WHERE indicates the content/file that can be found in your table.

Without the WHERE key word, your SQL query would be 'lost in space' not knowing what data to filter and select.

You can use the following steps to filter your data.

Steps #1 – Decide what data to filter

Know specifically what date in your table you would like to filter. Once you have decided, go to the next step.

Steps #2 – Select the data

Write your SQL query with the key word SELECT to indicate your selected data.

Make sure you have chosen properly. Inaccuracies in your query can produce wrong results.

You can write the SQL query like this:

Example: SELECT "column_name1, 'column_name2, "column_name3"

Remember to separate the column names with commas.

Using the table displayed below, compose your SQL query based on the stated premise.

Let's say you have chosen to filter all students below age 17, and want to display all students, who are older than 17.

How would you write your SQL statement?

Students

StudentNo	LastName	FirstName	Age	Address	City
1	Potter	Michael	17	130 Reed Ave.	Cheyenne
2	Walker	Jean	18	110 Westlake	Cody
3	Anderson	Ted	18	22 Staten Sq.	Laramie
4	Dixon	Allan	18	12 Glenn	Casper

				Rd.	
5	Cruise	Timothy	19	20 Reed Ave.	Cheyenne
6	Depp	Adam	17	276 Grand Ave.	Laramie
7	Lambert	David	19	32 8th St.	Cody
8	Cowell	Janine	18	140 Center St.	Casper
9	Kennedy	Daniel	17	11 21st St.	Laramie
10	Budzinak	Leila	20	24 Wing St.	Cheyenne

You can write the SQL query like this:

> Example: SELECT LastName, FirstName, Address, City

Step #3 – Indicate FROM what table the data came from

After selecting the columns you want displayed, indicate FROM what table they should come from.

> Example: Example: SELECT LastName, FirstName, Address, City FROM Students

Step #4 – Add the WHERE clause

This is significant in filtering data, so remember to always use the WHERE clause. What data do you want to filter?

In the above exercise, you want to display all students above the age of 17. Hence, your resulting SQL statement would appear like this.

Example: SELECT LastName, FirstName, Address, City FROM students WHERE Age = > 17;

Step #5 – Always add the semicolon

SQL queries or statement almost always end with a semicolon. The semicolon is already added to the example above.

More examples and exercises will be given in the next chapters.

Chapter 19: Creating Indexes

Creating indexes is also a basic knowledge that you should learn as a SQL beginner.

These indexes are important when searching for data or tables because they provide a prompt and efficient result to queries.

To save time and effort, create indexes only for tables that you often use.

The basic CREATE INDEX SQL query is:

Example: CREATE INDEX "Index_name"

ON "table_name"; (you can include the
"colum_name", if you   need that data)

Example: CREATE INDEX Studex

ON Students (Name, Age, City);

The SQL above will display all files - even duplicate files. If you want your result table to display only unique data, you can use the keywords CREATE UNIQUE INDEX, instead.

The basic SQL statement is similar with that of CREATE INDEX.

Here it is:

Example: CREATE UNIQUE INDEX "Index_name"

ON "table_name"; (you can include the "colum_name", if you   need that data)

Retrieve your tables quickly by using CREATE INDEX.

Chapter 20: Using the WHERE Clause

The use of the WHERE clause is crucial in creating SQL queries. Without the WHERE clause, some queries or statements cannot be completed. It is mostly used in filtering data, which is discussed in another chapter.

Here are the various functions of the WHERE clause:

1. It filters data. Only the columns that you have selected will be displayed in your output table.

   Example: SELECT "column_name1", "column_name2", "column_name3"

         FROM "table_name"

         WHERE "column_name" operator value;

   Let's say this is your base table,

   BookSales

Name	Age	City	Book	Price
De Leon Dina	45	Canberra	Fiction	50.00
Danes Joan	24	Detroit	NonFiction	120.00
Lannister Ted	34	Grand Rapids	Fiction	60.00

Jahangiri Tom	43	San Antonio	Fiction	20.00
Mitchell Ben	29	Laramie	Fiction	30.00

And you want to display the columns for Name, City and Book only, you will be creating a SQL query in this manner:

Example: SELECT *

FROM BookSales

WHERE Book = 'Fiction';

Your resulting table (output) would appear this way:

BookSales

Name	Age	City	Book	Price
De Leon Dina	45	Canberra	Fiction	50.00
Lannister Ted	34	Grand Rapids	Fiction	60.00
Jahangiri Tom	43	San Antonio	Fiction	20.00
Mitchell Ben	29	Laramie	Fiction	30.00

Remember the * symbol, which indicates all column.

2. It can filter data for text fields versus numeric fields.

Example: SELECT *

FROM BookSales

WHERE Price <= 50;

Remember that numbers are not enclosed in single quotes, only letter strings are, such as, 'Canberra', 'Laramie'.

If you use the base table as your input table, the SQL syntax above will produce the table below.

BookSales

Name	Age	City	Book	Price
De Leon Dina	45	Canberra	Fiction	50.00
Jahangiri Tom	43	San Antonio	Fiction	20.00
Mitchell Ben	29	Laramie	Fiction	30.00

3. It can be used to retrieve or fetch data from your databases

Example: SELECT Name, Age, Book, Price

FROM BookSales

WHERE Age >20;

Using the base table and applying the SQL syntax with the WHERE clause, you will come up with this result table:

BookSales

Name	Age	Book	Price
De Leon Dina	45	Fiction	50.00
Danes Joan	24	NonFiction	120.00
Lannister Ted	34	Fiction	60.00
Jahangiri Tom	43	Fiction	20.00
Mitchell Ben	29	Fiction	30.00

4. **It can be used with character operators such as, LIKE, NOT, IN, and many more.** You can refer to chapters 27 & 33 for discussions on the most commonly used operators.

Example: SELECT *

FROM BookSales

WHERE Name LIKE d%;

The d% symbol indicates that you are selecting values in the name column that begin with the letter d. The %

symbol denotes wildcards (missing letters). You can refer to **chapter 21** for more information.

Based on the base table and the SQL statement in #4, your output table would be this:

BookSales

Name	Age	City	Book	Price
De Leon Dina	45	Canberra	Fiction	50.00
Danes Joan	24	Detroit	NonFiction	120.00

Here are more examples:

1. **Using the WHERE clause with the UPDATE keyword.**

   Example: UPDATE BookSales

   SET City = 'Canberra'

   WHERE Age = 24

Based on the original table, the resulting table would be this:

BookSales

Name	Age	City	Book	Price
De Leon Dina	45	Canberra	Fiction	50.00
Danes Joan	24	Canberra	NonFiction	120.00
Lannister	34	Grand	Fiction	60.00

Ted		Rapids		
Jahangiri Tom	43	San Antonio	Fiction	20.00
Mitchell Ben	29	Laramie	Fiction	30.00

2. Using the WHERE clause with UPDATE

Example: UPDATE BookSales

SET Price=50

WHERE Name = 'Lannister Ted';

Using the base table to apply the SQL query to, this would be the resulting table.

BookSales

Name	Age	City	Book	Price
De Leon Dina	45	Canberra	Fiction	50.00
Danes Joan	24	Detroit	NonFiction	120.00
Lannister Ted	34	Grand Rapids	Fiction	50.00
Jahangiri Tom	43	San Antonio	Fiction	20.00
Mitchell Ben	29	Laramie	Fiction	30.00

Another example:

UPDATE BookSales

SET City = 'San Antonio', Age = 34

WHERE Names = 'Danes Joan';

The SET clause specifies what changes or updates you would like to do, while the WHERE clause identifies where you want those changes done. Hence with the SQL statement above, you want to UPDATE the data in your BookSales table by changing the City and Age entries on Danes Joan.

So, the resulting table will appear like this:

BookSales

Name	Age	City	Book	Price
De Leon Dina	45	Canberra	Fiction	50.00
Danes Joan	34	San Antonio	NonFiction	120.00
Lannister Ted	34	Grand Rapids	Fiction	60.00
Jahangiri Tom	43	San Antonio	Fiction	20.00
Mitchell Ben	29	Laramie	Fiction	30.00

The WHERE clause is essential in UPDATING your data because without it, all of your columns will be UPDATED with the same values.

The WHERE clause can also be used in the AND and OR keywords such as, the example below:

Example: SELECT *

FROM BookSales

WHERE City = 'San Antonio'

AND Age >40;

Using the base table, your resulting table would be:

BookSales

Name	Age	City	Book	Price
Jahangiri Tom	43	San Antonio	Fiction	20.00

Example: SELECT *

FROM BookSales

WHERE City = 'Laramie'

OR City= 'Grand Rapids';

Using the base table, the resulting output would be this:

BookSales

Name	Age	City	Book	Price
Lannister Ted	34	Grand Rapids	Fiction	60.00
Mitchell Ben	29	Laramie	Fiction	30.00

Example: SELECT *

FROM BookSales

WHERE Book = 'Fiction'

AND (City = 'Laramie' OR City = 'Canberra');

Using the base table, the output table will appear this way:

BookSales

Name	Age	City	Book	Price
De Leon Dina	45	Canberra	Fiction	50.00
Mitchell Ben	29	Laramie	Fiction	30.00

There are more examples of the WHERE clause or keyword in the various chapters.

Chapter 21: Using TRANSACTIONS

A TRANSACTION is any task done against tables or files in a database. These transactions may range from simple to complex tasks, but whatever it is, you should ensure the reliability, integrity and credibility of your database.

Examples of transactions are; dropping, deleting, updating, joining tables, modifying and all the activities that you perform with your databases.

A single transaction may involve several tasks in one go.

That is why you have to know what to do in cases when there is system failure or there are aborted tasks.

There are commands that you must be familiar with if you want to protect your databases.

SAVEPOINT COMMAND

This command is used when you want to go back to some point in your transaction without having to go back all the way to the very first activity. This will save time and effort.

The SQL statement for SAVEPOINT COMMAND is:

Example: SAVEPOINT SAVEPOINT_name;

ROLLBACK COMMAND

This command is useful when you would like to go back (roll back) to a point in the transaction that has not been saved yet in your database.

You cannot make another ROLLBACK COMMAND to a transaction that has already used the command.

The SQL statement for ROLLBACK COMMAND is:

Example: ROLLBACK;

As an example let's use the table below as our base table:

StudenInformation

StudentNo	Year	Average
1	1st	90
2	1st	87
3	3rd	88
4	5th	77
5	2nd	93
6	1st	88
7	1st	80
8	2nd	79
9	3rd	94
10	4th	80

Example: DELETE Average

FROM StudentInformation

WHERE StudentNo=5;

ROLLBACK;

Table-output is the same because of the ROLLBACK COMMAND:

StudentInformation

StudentNo	Year	Average
1	1st	90
2	1st	87
3	3rd	88
4	5th	77
5	2nd	93
6	1st	88
7	1st	80

8	2nd	79
9	3rd	94
10	4th	80

This SQL statement will first perform the first command, which is deleting the StudentNo with a value of 5, when you add the ROLLBACK COMMAND, the table will roll back to that point and will display the same results.

COMMIT COMMAND

The COMMIT COMMAND indicates that your transactions have been committed or saved to the database.

The SQL statement for the COMMIT COMMAND is simple:

Example: COMMIT;

Using the base table above, let's have specific examples.

Example: DELETE FROM Students

WHERE Average = 77;

COMMIT;

Based on the SQL query above and the original tables, the resulting table would look like this:

StudenInformation

StudentNo	Year	Average
1	1st	90

2	1st	87
3	3rd	88
5	2nd	93
6	1st	88
7	1st	80
8	2nd	79
9	3rd	94
10	4th	80

The row with a Grade = 77 was deleted and then COMMITTED (saved).

SET TRANSACTION COMMAND

This command is used to set the transaction that you have selected. The SQL statement for this SET TRANSACTION COMMAND is:

Example: SET TRANSACTION [read only];

Or

Example: SET TRANSACTION [read write];

RELEASE SAVEPOINT COMMAND

This command is used when you would like to remove a previous SAVEPOINT that you have created.

The SQL query for this command is:

Example: RELEASE SAVEPOINT SAVEPOINT_name;

Rolling back the transaction, after you have released the SAVEPOINT, is no longer possible. You have to perform the SQL according to the query on updating or modifying tables.

PROPERTIES OF TRANSACTIONS

There are certain PROPERTIES OF TRANSACTIONS that you should be aware of such as:

- **Consistency**

  This Indicates that the databases have changed consistently, after you have performed a transaction. If your database has an efficient DBMS, there will be no problem with the consistency of your transactions.

- **Durability**

  As the term implies, the data in your database remain 'durable' or unaltered in cases of system failure. They are durable like the branded Puma rubber shoes that many people wear. This is just to make a point.

- **Isolation**

  This indicates that transactions can function independently but, at the same time transparent. This is important when you want to work quicker and more efficiently.

- **Atomicity**

  Atomicity is one way by which the databases can protect themselves. This is because when there is task failure, it will abort the task and the transaction will ROLL BACK to its previous state. It ensures that all tasks within the transactions are done properly. This will ensure success in all the transactions that you have initiated.

You can transact successfully by using all the pointers above. You can do a quick read later when you encounter some problems with your SQL syntax.

Chapter 22: Using the TRUNCATE TABLE COMMAND

The TRUNCATE TABLE COMMAND is used when you want to delete data from a table that is already existing. This means you do not have plans of deleting the table, but only the contents.

While deleting the table can be quicker, it is not advisable because you might need the table format later on. Hence, TRUNCATING TABLE is the best option for you because the table is still there and all you have to do is enter the data once you have them.

The SQL statement for TRUNCATE TABLE is:

Example: TRUNCATE TABLE "table_name";

Using the base table in the previous chapter, which is, StudentInformation, you can now TRUNCATE this table with this SQL statement above.

StudenInformation

StudentNo	Year	Average
1	1st	90
2	1st	87
3	3rd	88
5	2nd	93
6	1st	88

7	1st	80
8	2nd	79
9	3rd	94
10	4th	80

Example: TRUNCATE TABLE StudentInformation;

This would be the result when you perform the SELECT keyword for the table.

Example: Empty set (0.00 sec)

Keep in mind that you can revive the table again and use it when you deem it appropriate.

Chapter 23: Using ORDER BY Clause

This chapter is focused on the use of the SQL key word ORDER BY. This clause is used to sort out the retrieved data or results displayed, after you have submitted your query.

It is a powerful keyword that can allow you to manipulate and edit the displayed results to suit your preferences.

The specific uses of the clause ORDER BY are the following:

1. **It can sort results in ascending order.**

    Example: SELECT "column_name"

    FROM "table_name"

    ORDER BY "column_name" ASC;

2. **It can sort results in descending order**

    Example: SELECT "column_name"

    FROM "table_name"

    ORDER BY "column_name" DESC;

3. **It can sort several specified columns**

    Example: SELECT *

FROM "table_name"

ORDER BY "column_name1", "column_name2", "column_name3";

Using the table below, compose your SQL syntax that are specified.

Students

StudentNo	Names	Age	Address	City
1	Potter, Michael	17	130 Reed Ave.	Cheyenne
2	Walker, Jean	18	110 Westlake	Cody
3	Anderson, Ted	18	22 Staten Sq.	Laramie
4	Dixon, Allan	18	12 Glenn Rd.	Casper
5	Cruise, Timothy	19	20 Reed Ave.	Cheyenne
6	Depp, Adam	17	276 Grand Ave.	Laramie
7	Lambert, David	19	32 8th St.	Cody

8	Cowell, Janine	18	140 Center St.	Casper
9	Kennedy, Daniel	17	11 21st St.	Laramie
10	Budzinak, Leila	20	24 Wing St.	Cheyenne

EXERCISES

Compose the SQL statements for the following:

Exercise #1- Sort the City in ascending order

Exercise #2 - Sort the Names in ascending order

Exercise #3 - Sort the Age from the youngest to the oldest student

Exercise #4 – Sort the Age from the oldest to the youngest student

Try composing your SQL statements before looking at the answers.

ANSWERS

Exercise #1

SELECT *

FROM Students

ORDER BY City ASC;

Using the base table, your resulting table will appear this way:

Students

StudentNo	Names	Age	Address	City
4	Dixon, Allan	18	12 Glenn Rd.	Casper
8	Cowell, Janine	18	140 Center St.	Casper
1	Potter, Michael	17	130 Reed Ave.	Cheyenne
5	Cruise, Timothy	19	20 Reed Ave.	Cheyenne
10	Budzinak, Leila	20	24 Wing St.	Cheyenne
2	Walker, Jean	18	110 Westlake	Cody
7	Lambert, David	19	32 8th St.	Cody
3	Anderson, Ted	18	22 Staten Sq.	Laramie
6	Depp, Adam	17	276 Grand Ave.	Laramie
9	Kennedy, Daniel	17	11 21st St.	Laramie

Exercise #2

SELECT *

FROM Students

ORDER BY Names DESC;

Using the base table, your resulting table will appear this way:

Students

StudentNo	Names	Age	Address	City
2	Walker, Jean	18	110 Westlake	Cody
1	Potter, Michael	17	130 Reed Ave.	Cheyenne
7	Lambert, David	19	32 8th St.	Cody
9	Kennedy, Daniel	17	11 21st St.	Laramie
4	Dixon, Allan	18	12 Glenn Rd.	Casper
6	Depp, Adam	17	276 Grand Ave.	Laramie
5	Cruise, Timothy	19	20 Reed Ave.	Cheyenne
8	Cowell, Janine	18	140 Center St.	Casper
10	Budzinak, Leila	20	24 Wing St.	Cheyenne
3	Anderson, Ted	18	22 Staten Sq.	Laramie

Exercise #3

SELECT *

FROM Students

ORDER BY Age ASC;

Using the base table, your output table will appear this way:

Students

StudentNo	Names	Age	Address	City
1	Potter, Michael	17	130 Reed Ave.	Cheyenne
9	Kennedy, Daniel	17	11 21st St.	Laramie
6	Depp, Adam	17	276 Grand Ave.	Laramie
2	Walker, Jean	18	110 Westlake	Cody
4	Dixon, Allan	18	12 Glenn Rd.	Casper
8	Cowell, Janine	18	140 Center St.	Casper
3	Anderson, Ted	18	22 Staten Sq.	Laramie
7	Lambert, David	19	32 8th St.	Cody
5	Cruise, Timothy	19	20 Reed Ave.	Cheyenne
10	Budzinak, Leila	20	24 Wing St.	Cheyenne

Exercise #4

SELECT *

FROM Students

ORDER BY Age DESC;

Using the base table, your resulting table will appear this way:

Students

StudentNo	Names	Age	Address	City
10	Budzinak, Leila	20	24 Wing St.	Cheyenne
7	Lambert, David	19	32 8th St.	Cody
5	Cruise, Timothy	19	20 Reed Ave.	Cheyenne
2	Walker, Jean	18	110 Westlake	Cody
4	Dixon, Allan	18	12 Glenn Rd.	Casper
8	Cowell, Janine	18	140 Center St.	Casper
3	Anderson, Ted	18	22 Staten Sq.	Laramie
1	Potter, Michael	17	130 Reed Ave.	Cheyenne
9	Kennedy, Daniel	17	11 21st St.	Laramie
6	Depp, Adam	17	276 Grand Ave.	Laramie

As you experience using the ORDER BY clause, you will surely enjoy creating your SQL statements.

Chapter 24: Using NULL VALUES

You can use the NULL VALUES whenever appropriate. The NULL values appear when the data are missing or unknown.

Hence, the default value in tables, where there are no DATA retrieved, is NULL. There are two types of NULL VALUES, the IS NULL and IS NOT NULL.

NULL VALUES are unlike numbers because they do not have a numerical value. A NULL VALUE is different from 0, so you cannot use the comparison operators namely, <, >, =, and so on, to test its value. Therefore, how can we determine the NULL VALUES?

Here's how:

Use the IS NULL and IS NOT NULL operators.

If the table below is your base table:

Students

StudentNo	Names	Age	Address	City
1	Potter, Michael	17	130 Reed Ave.	Cheyenne
2	Walker, Jean	18	110 Westlake	Cody
3	Anderson, Ted		22 Staten Sq.	Laramie
4	Dixon, Allan	18	12 Glenn Rd.	Casper

5	Cruise, Timothy	19	20 Reed Ave.	Cheyenne
6	Depp, Adam		276 Grand Ave.	Laramie
7	Lambert, David		32 8th St.	Cody
8	Cowell, Janine	18	140 Center St.	Casper
9	Kennedy, Daniel		11 21st St.	Laramie
10	Budzinak, Leila		24 Wing St.	Cheyenne

And you want to select all the NULL VALUES in the Age column, you can write your SQL query this way:

Example: SELECT Names, Age, Address, City

FROM Students

WHERE Age IS NULL;

Your SQL statement will retrieve the data with your result-table appearing like this:

Students

Names	Age	Address	City
Anderson, Ted		22 Staten Sq.	Laramie

Depp, Adam		276 Grand Ave.	Laramie
Lambert, David		32 8th St.	Cody
Kennedy, Daniel		11 21st St.	Laramie
Budzinak, Leila		24 Wing St.	Cheyenne

All the entries without values are retrieved or displayed together with the columns that you have specified.

Another example is this:

Example: SELECT *

FROM Students

WHERE Age IS NULL;

Using the base table, the output or resulting table will appear this way:

Students

StudentNo	Names	Age	Address	City
3	Anderson, Ted		22 Staten Sq.	Laramie
6	Depp, Adam		276 Grand Ave.	Laramie

7	Lambert, David		32 8th St.	Cody
9	Kennedy, Daniel		11 21st St.	Laramie
10	Budzinak, Leila		24 Wing St.	Cheyenne

Use IS NOT NULL

IS NOT NULL is used when you want to fetch the columns that have no NULL VALUES.

Your SQL syntax will be this:

Example: SELECT Names, Age, Address, City

FROM Students

WHERE Age IS NOT NULL;

Using the base table in this chapter, your resulting table would be:

Students

Names	Age	Address	City
Potter, Michael	17	130 Reed Ave.	Cheyenne
Walker, Jean	18	110 Westlake	Cody
Dixon, Allan	18	12 Glenn Rd.	Casper

| Cruise, Timothy | 19 | 20 Reed Ave. | Cheyenne |
| Cowell, Janine | 18 | 140 Center St. | Casper |

Another example is this:

Example: SELECT *

FROM Students

WHERE Age IS NOT NULL;

Using the base table, your output table will be:

Students

StudentNo	Names	Age	Address	City
1	Potter, Michael	17	130 Reed Ave.	Cheyenne
2	Walker, Jean	18	110 Westlake	Cody
4	Dixon, Allan	18	12 Glenn Rd.	Casper
5	Cruise, Timothy	19	20 Reed Ave.	Cheyenne
8	Cowell, Janine	18	140 Center St.	Casper

Take note that when you use the * sign, all the columns in the table are selected.

Chapter 25: Using NULL FUNCTIONS

Since you have learned about the IS NULL and IS NOT NULL values, you must also learn the NULL FUNCTIONS to maximize the use of the NULL VALUES.

There are four most common NULL FUNCTIONS. These are:

1. **IFNULL ()**

2. **ISNULL ()**

3. **NVL ()**

4. **COALESCE ()**

The function of each will be disclosed in the examples below.

We will use a new base table with the examples because the above-mentioned functions are useful in numerical tables.

BookSales

BookNo	Price	Sold	TotalSales
1	45.00	3	135.00
2	130.00	5	650.00
3	49.00	70	3430.00
4	60.00		
5	100.00		
6	75.00	50	3750.00
7	250.00	89	22250.00

In the table above, you will notice that there are some NULL VALUES. Some software may not be able to compute, if there are no specified values in some of the columns, so you have to add a value.

In the base table above, we can assign 0 as the value of NULL, so that we can fill in the blanks, leaving no blanks in the columns.

Here's how you can do it:

For MySQL

> Example: SELECT BookNo, Sold*(Price+IFNULL(TotalSales,0))
>
> FROM BookSales;

This SQL query will result to this table:

BookSales

BookNo	Price	Sold	TotalSales
1	45.00	3	135.00
2	130.00	5	650.00
3	49.00	70	3430.00
4	60.00	0	0

5	100.00	0	0
6	75.00	50	3750.00
7	250.00	89	22250.00

The COALESCE () of MySQL can also be used this way:

Example: SELECT BookNo, Sold*(Price+COALESCE(TotalSales,0))

FROM BookSales;

For MS (Microsoft) Access

In MS Access, there is a little difference in the SQL statement.

Example: SELECT BookNo,
Sold*(Price+IF(ISNULL(TotalSales),0, (TotalSales));

FROM BookSales;

BookSales

BookNo	Price	Sold	TotalSales
1	45.00	3	135.00
2	130.00	5	650.00
3	49.00	70	3430.00
4	60.00	0	0
5	100.00	0	0

6	75.00	50	3750.00
7	250.00	89	22250.00

Basically the same table will result from the SQL query.

For ORACLE

We have to use the NVL () because the ISNULL function could not be performed. But the result-table is the same.

Example: SELECT BookNo,
Sold*(Price+NVL(TotalSales,0));

FROM BookSales;

This produces the same table with the SQL statement.

For SQL

SELECT BookNo,
Sold*(Price+ISNULL(TotalSales,0))

FROM BookSales;

This will also produce the same table as the other methods.

Chapter 26: Using the ALTER TABLE Query

There will be several times you need to use the ALTER TABLE command. This is when you need to edit, delete or modify tables and constraints.

The basic SQL statement for this query is:

> Example: ALTER TABLE "table_name"
>
> ADD "column_name" data type;

You can use this base table as your demo table:

Traffic_hs2064

Country	Searchword	Time	Post
America	perfect	5	Matchmaker
Italy	partner	2	NatureTripping
Sweden	mate	10	Fiction
Spain	couple	3	News
Malaysia	team	6	Health
Philippines	island	5	Entertainment
Africa	lover	4	Opinion

If your base table is the table above, and you want to add another column labeled City, you can create your SQL query this way:

Examples: ALTER TABLE Traffic_hs2064

ADD City char(30);

The output table would appear this way:

Traffic_hs2064

Country	Searchword	Time	Post	City
America	perfect	5	Matchmaker	NULL
Italy	partner	2	NatureTripping	NULL
Sweden	mate	10	Fiction	NULL
Spain	couple	3	News	NULL
Malaysia	team	6	Health	NULL
Philippines	island	5	Entertainment	NULL

Africa	lover	4	Opinion	NULL

You can also ALTER a table to ADD a constraint such as, NOT NULL.

Example: ALTER TABLE Traffic_hs2064

MODIFY City datatype NOT NULL;

This will modify all entries that are NOT NULL.

You can also ALTER TABLE to DROP COLUMNS such as, the example below:

Example: ALTER TABLE Traffic_hs2064 DROP COLUMN Time;

Using the second table with this SQL query, the resulting table will be this:

Traffic_hs2064

Country	Searchword	Post	City
America	perfect	Matchmaker	NULL
Italy	partner	NatureTripping	NULL
Sweden	mate	Fiction	NULL
Spain	couple	News	NULL
Malaysia	team	Health	NULL
Philippines	island	Entertainment	NULL
Africa	lover	Opinion	NULL

You can ALTER TABLE by adding a UNIQUE CONSTRAINT. You can construct your SQL query this way:

Example: ALTER TABLE Traffic_hs2064

ADD CONSTRAINT uc_Country UNIQUE (Country, SearchWord);

In addition to these uses, the ALTER TABLE can also be used with the DROP CONSTRAINT like the example below.

Example: ALTER TABLE Traffic_hs2064

DROP CONSTRAINT uc_City;

Here are examples of CONSTRAINTS.

- **NOT NULL**

This constraint indicates that the NOT NULL values should not be present in the columns of a stored table.

- **CHECK**

  This will ensure that all parameters have values that have met the criteria.

- **UNIQUE**

  This ascertains that all values in the columns are distinct or unique.

- **PRIMARY KEY**

  This indicates that the values in two or more columns are NOT NULL and simultaneously UNIQUE.

- **FOREIGN KEY**

  This will ascertain that the values of columns from different tables match.

- **DEFAULT**

  There is a specified DEFAULT value for columns. This may appear as blanks or appear as NULL.

Make sure you use these constraints properly to make the most out of your SQL queries.

Chapter 27: Using BETWEEN Operator

The BETWEEN operator is usually used with numbers and dates, when you want to choose values within a certain range. Texts can also use the operator, BETWEEN.

The results displayed by a BETWEEN operator, can vary for different databases. In some databases, the selected columns may include the first value and the second value in its output, while some databases will exclude them.

There may also be a possibility when the first value is included in the output table, but not the second value specified. Hence, you may want to double check the outputs before finalizing your tables.

The BETWEEN operator can be used in a SQL query in the following manner.

Example: SELECT "column_name" (can be many columns)

FROM "table_name"

WHERE "column_name" BETWEEN "value1" AND "value2";

You can also write the SQL query this way, if you want to include all the columns.

Example: SELECT *

FROM "table_name"

WHERE "column_name" BETWEEN "value1" AND "value2";

Using the sample table below on Employees_Salary, compose your BETWEEN SQL syntax.

Employees_Salary

Names	Age	Salary	City
Williams, Michael	22	30000.00	Casper
Colton, Jean	24	37000.00	San Diego
Anderson, Ted	30	45000.00	Laramie
Dixon, Allan	27	43000.00	Chicago
Clarkson, Tim	25	35000.00	New York
Alaina, Ann	32	41000.00	Ottawa
Rogers, David	29	50000.00	San Francisco
Lambert, Jancy	38	47000.00	Los Angeles

Kennedy, Tom	27	34000.00	Denver
Schultz, Diana	40	46000.00	New York

Example: SELECT *

FROM Employees_Salary

WHERE Age BETWEEN 22 AND 30;

The SQL statement above will produce this table:

Employees_Salary

Names	Age	Salary	City
Williams, Michael	22	30000.00	Casper
Colton, Jean	24	37000.00	San Diego
Anderson, Ted	30	45000.00	Laramie
Dixon, Allan	27	43000.00	Chicago
Clarkson, Tim	25	35000.00	New York
Rogers, David	29	50000.00	San Francisco
Kennedy, Tom	27	34000.00	Denver

Another version of the BETWEEN operator is the NOT BETWEEN.

This SQL key word will display the content of the table that are outside the range of the specified values.

Example: SELECT *

FROM Employees_Salary

WHERE Age NOT BETWEEN 22 AND 30;

The output of the SQL statement above is the table below:

Employees_Salary

Names	Age	Salary	City
Alaina, Ann	32	41000.00	Ottawa
Lambert, Jancy	38	47000.00	Los Angeles
Schultz, Diana	40	46000.00	New York

The SQL key words BETWEEN and NOT BETWEEN are essential especially for numbers.

Know how to use the BETWEEN operator well to create your tables.

However, take note that these keywords can also be used with text values.

For this SQL queries, the sample table is this.

Employees_Salary

Names	Age	Salary	City
Williams, Michael	22	30000.00	Casper
Colton, Jean	24	37000.00	San Diego
Anderson, Ted	30	45000.00	Laramie
Dixon, Allan	27	43000.00	Chicago
Clarkson, Tim	25	35000.00	New York
Alaina, Ann	32	41000.00	Ottawa
Rogers, David	29	50000.00	San Francisco
Lambert, Jancy	38	47000.00	Los Angeles
Kennedy, Tom	27	34000.00	Denver
Schultz, Diana	40	46000.00	New York

Let's say you want your output or result table to display all cities beginning with any of the letters between 'B' and 'D', you can express your SQL statement this way.

Example: SELECT *

FROM Employees_Salary

WHERE City BETWEEN 'B' AND 'D';

Your result or output from the SQL query above will be the table below.

Employees_Salary

Names	Age	Salary	City
Williams, Michael	22	30000.00	Casper
Dixon, Allan	27	43000.00	Chicago
Kennedy, Tom	27	34000.00	Denver

For the use of the NOT BETWEEN key word or operator, you can follow the same statement with the number values.

Example: SELECT *

FROM Employees_Salary

WHERE City NOT BETWEEN 'B' AND 'D';

Remember to enclose your letters within single quotes. This is important to make your SQL query complete.

If you use the same original table above, your output with the SQL syntax would be the table below.

Employees_Salary

Names	Age	Salary	City
Colton, Jean	24	37000.00	San Diego
Anderson, Ted	30	45000.00	Laramie
Clarkson, Tim	25	35000.00	New York
Alaina, Ann	32	41000.00	Ottawa
Rogers, David	29	50000.00	San Francisco
Lambert, Jancy	38	47000.00	Los Angeles
Schultz, Diana	40	46000.00	New York

You can also use BETWEEN with IN to exclude certain entries that you don't want to display.

From the sample table below:

Employees_Salary

Names	Age	Salary	City
Williams, Michael	22	30000.00	Casper

Colton, Jean	24	37000.00	San Diego
Anderson, Ted	30	45000.00	Laramie
Dixon, Allan	27	43000.00	Chicago
Clarkson, Tim	25	35000.00	New York
Alaina, Ann	32	41000.00	Ottawa
Rogers, David	29	50000.00	San Francisco
Lambert, Jancy	38	47000.00	Los Angeles
Kennedy, Tom	27	34000.00	Denver
Schultz, Diana	40	46000.00	New York

Let's say you want to display in your output table all the cities with any of the letters between 'B' and 'D', but not those who are aged 22, 23 and 24.

This is how you express your SQL statement;

    Example: SELECT *

        FROM Employees_Salary

        WHERE (City BETWEEN 'B' AND 'D')

        AND NOT Age IN (22, 23,24);

Your output or result would be the table below:

Employees_Salary

Names	Age	Salary	City
Anderson, Ted	30	45000.00	Laramie
Clarkson, Tim	25	35000.00	New York
Alaina, Ann	32	41000.00	Ottawa
Rogers, David	29	50000.00	San Francisco
Lambert, Jancy	38	47000.00	Los Angeles
Schultz, Diana	40	46000.00	New York

You can also use the BETWEEN operator with date values. Your sample table is:

Employees_Salary

Names	Age	Salary	City	DateOfEntry
Colton, Jean	24	37000.00	San Diego	8/21/2015
Anderson, Ted	30	45000.00	Laramie	10/5/2014
Clarkson, Tim	25	35000.00	New York	6/6/2012
Alaina, Ann	32	41000.00	Ottawa	7/20/2010
Rogers, David	29	50000.00	San Francisco	9/25/2014
Lambert,	38	47000.00	Los	10/20/2013

			Angeles	
Jancy				
Schultz, Diana	40	46000.00	New York	3/5/2016

Here is an example:

Example: SELECT *

FROM Employees_Salary

WHERE DateOfEntry BETWEEN #07/20/2010# AND #06/20/2012#;

This SQL query will display the table below:

Employees_Salary

Names	Age	Salary	City	DateOfEntry
Clarkson, Tim	25	35000.00	New York	6/6/2012
Alaina, Ann	32	41000.00	Ottawa	7/20/2010

The BETWEEN clause is crucial, especially for numerical values, so remember to use this significant clause in your SQL statements.

Chapter 28: Using AND and OR

The AND and OR operators are important in SQL because they are used to create complex SQLs and to filter data based on one or more conditions.

To be more accurate, the AND operator is used when you want to display data or file that are true with both specified conditions.

On the other hand, the OR operator works the other way around, the keyword will display either of the specified data, record or file.

Using AND

Let's say your base or original table is this:

Employees_Salary

Names	Age	Salary	City	DateOfEntry
Colton, Jean	24	37000.00	San Diego	8/21/2015
Anderson, Ted	30	45000.00	Laramie	10/5/2014
Clarkson, Tim	25	35000.00	New York	6/6/2012
Alaina, Ann	32	41000.00	Ottawa	7/20/2010
Rogers, David	29	50000.00	San Francisco	9/25/2014

| Lambert, Jancy | 38 | 47000.00 | Los Angeles | 10/20/2013 |
| Schultz, Diana | 40 | 46000.00 | New York | 3/5/2016 |

And you want your resulting table to display both the Age of those below 30 and those who live in New York, your SQL query would be:

Example: SELECT *

FROM Employees_Salary

WHERE Age = < 30

AND City = 'New York';

Employees_Salary

Names	Age	Salary	City	DateOfEntry
Clarkson, Tim	25	35000.00	New York	6/6/2012

Using OR

With the same base table above, create an SQL making use of the same parameter/files, but using the OR operator.

Example: SELECT *

FROM Employees_Salary

WHERE City = 'New York'

OR City = "San Diego';

The resulting table or data output would be the table below.

Employees_Salary

Names	Age	Salary	City	DateOfEntry
Colton, Jean	24	37000.00	San Diego	8/21/2015
Clarkson, Tim	25	35000.00	New York	6/6/2012
Schultz, Diana	40	46000.00	New York	3/5/2016

Combining AND and OR operators

Combining your AND and OR operators can help you create more tables according to your preferences. Remember to use the parenthesis in complex SQL statements or expressions.

These are examples on how to use your AND and OR operators. Try some of these exercises.

Base table

Employees_Salary

Names	Age	Salary	City	DateOfEntry
Colton, Jean	24	37000.00	San Diego	8/21/2015
Anderson, Ted	30	45000.00	Laramie	10/5/2014
Clarkson, Tim	25	35000.00	New York	6/6/2012
Alaina, Ann	32	41000.00	Ottawa	7/20/2010
Rogers, David	29	50000.00	San Francisco	9/25/2014
Lambert, Jancy	38	47000.00	Los Angeles	10/20/2013
Schultz, Diana	40	46000.00	New York	3/5/2016

Example: SELECT * FROM Employees_Salary

WHERE City = 'San Diego'

AND (Age = 24 OR Age = 26);

Your output or resulting table would appear like this:

Employees_Salary

Names	Age	Salary	City	DateOfEntry
Colton, Jean	24	37000.00	San Diego	8/21/2015

Learn more in using your AND and OR operators by doing some exercises with your own tables.

There are more examples given in the chapter for the WHERE clause.

Chapter 29: Using SELECT DISTINCT Query

Another SQL keyword that you should know is the SELECT DISTINCT statement.

There is a difference between a SELECT statement from a SELECT DISTINCT statement or query.

The SELECT statement will display all files even if there are similar contents, while the SELECT DISTINCT statement will only display values or content that are unique, different or distinct.

This the basic SELECT DISTINCT query.

Example: SELECT   DISTINCT   "column_name1", "column_name2", "column_name3"

FROM "table_name";

If you have the table below:

Online_Students

Name	Age	City	Country
Pollack, Leni	25	Anchorage	United States
Cooper, Brian	18	Atlanta	United States
Urban, Ned	56	Manila	Philippines
Lowell, Cathy	45	Madrid	Spain

Moore, Virginia	18	Seoul	South Korea

And you want to display DISTINCT values of Age from your Online_Students table, you can express your SQL query this way:

Example: SELECT   DISTINCT   Age   from Online_Students;

Your resulting table would appear this way. There are two 18 entries, so only one entry appears, and the duplicate entry is excluded.

Online_Students

Age
18
25
56
45

You may want to include the names, so you express your SQL query this way:

Example: SELECT DISTINCT Name, City

FROM Online_Students;

Your resulting table or output would be this table, since all the entries are DISTINCT, your values will all appear in your output.

Online_Students

Name	City
Pollack, Leni	Anchorage
Cooper, Brian	Atlanta
Urban, Ned	Manila
Lowell, Cathy	Madrid
Moore, Virginia	Seoul

If you want to SELECT DISTINCT Name and Age from the same table, your SQL query would read:

Example: SELECT DISTINCT Name, Age

FROM Online_students;

Your resulting table would be:

Online_Students

Name	Age
Pollack, Leni	25
Cooper, Brian	18

Urban, Ned	56
Lowell, Cathy	45
Moore, Virginia	18

Take note that in the Age column, there are two Age 18 entries, but they are both displayed or retrieved on the new table because both their Names are DISTINCT.

Just remember that the DISTINCT keyword or statement removes duplicates on the specified columns.

Chapter 30: Using SELECT TOP

The use of SELECT TOP in SQL statements cannot be discounted due to the fact that it is very useful to retrieve a number of data from thousands of tables in the database.

There are slight differences in the SQL query, depending on the server used.

MySQL statement

You can create the basic SELECT TOP MySQL statement this way:

> Example: SELECT "column_name1", "column_name2",
>
> ...
>
> FROM "table_name"
>
> LIMIT number;

MS Access Statement

Usually, the basic SQL statement for MS Access is:

> Example: SELECT   TOP   number/percent "column_name1", "column_name2", "column_name3",
>
> ...
>
> FROM "table_name";

If your table is the table below:

Online_Students

Name	Age	City	Country
Pollack, Leni	25	Anchorage	United States
Cooper, Brian	18	Atlanta	United States
Urban, Ned	56	Manila	Philippines
Lowell, Cathy	45	Madrid	Spain
Moore, Virginia	18	Seoul	South Korea

And you want to the SELECT TOP 2, your SQL statement would be:

Example: SELECT TOP 2

FROM Online_Students;

The output would be the table below:

Online_Students

Name	Age	City	Country
Pollack, Leni	25	Anchorage	United States
Cooper, Brian	18	Atlanta	United States

ORACLE statement

Example: SELECT "column_name1" (you may add other columns)

FROM "table_name"

WHERE ROWNUM <= number;

Using the base table above, you can create your ORACLE statement this way:

Example: SELECT *

FROM Online_Students

WHERE ROWNUM <= 4;

Using the base table in this chapter, the resulting table will appear this way:

Online_Students

Name	Age	City	Country
Pollack, Leni	25	Anchorage	United States
Cooper, Brian	18	Atlanta	United States
Urban, Ned	56	Manila	Philippines
Lowell, Cathy	45	Madrid	Spain

The output table is the above table, since the value indicated is <=4.

This means that the ROWNUM (ROW NUMBER) is equal or less than 4.

Sometimes, the ROWNUM is used together with the ORDER BY clause:

Example: SELECT *

FROM Online_Students

WHERE ROWNUM <= 4

ORDER BY Name;

Using the base table, the resulting table is this. The Names were arranged first, and then the ROWNUM <=4 is applied.

Online_Students

Name	Age	City	Country
Cooper, Brian	18	Atlanta	United States
Lowell, Cathy	45	Madrid	Spain
Moore, Virginia	18	Seoul	South Korea
Pollack, Leni	25	Anchorage	United States

The ROWNUM is often used in ORACLE.

The WHERE clause and the ORDER BY clause can be interchanged in their positions in the SQL query. You will have to try both to see what comes out with the best results depending on the type of table you need.

Chapter 31: Using the LIKE Clause and WILDCARDS

The LIKE statement in SQL is typically used with WILDCARD operators. The use of the LIKE keyword is to compare a value or data with similar values.

The LIKE clause usually makes use of two WILDCARD operators namely: the underscore "_" and the percent (%) symbols.

The underscore indicates a single character or number, while the percent sign indicates several numbers or characters.

Here's an example of a basic SQL making use of LIKE and the WILDCARDS.

Example: SELECT FROM "table_name"

WHERE "column_name" LIKE '%value%' (or value%)

Example: SELECT FROM "table_name"

WHERE "column_name" LIKE 'value_' (or value_, or _value)

Take note that the value can be a number or a string. Also, depending on the table that you need, you can indicate whether the value that you want is found at the beginning, middle or end of the values.

Here are examples:

The SQL statements below are all based on this base table or demo table:

Employees_Salary

Names	Age	Salary	City
Williams, Michael	22	30000.00	Casper
Colton, Jean	24	37000.00	San Diego
Anderson, Ted	30	45000.00	Laramie
Dixon, Allan	27	43000.00	Chicago
Clarkson, Tim	25	35000.00	New York
Rogers, David	29	50000.00	San Francisco
Kennedy, Tom	27	34000.00	Denver

If you want to manipulate the data of the table above to compare the values in the Salary column, you can write your SQL statement this way:

Example: SELECT FROM Employees_Salary

WHERE Salary LIKE '%300%';

The above SQL query will display any Salary, where 300 is found in any position.

Applying the above query, the table output would be:

Employees_Salary

Names	Age	Salary	City
Williams, Michael	22	30000.00	Casper
Dixon, Allan	27	43000.00	Chicago

Example: SELECT FROM Employess_Salary

WHERE Salary LIKE '300%';

The position of the value (coming before the % sign) indicates that all Salaries starting with 300 will be displayed.

Using the base table above, the resulting table would be like this:

Employees_Salary

Names	Age	Salary	City
Williams, Michael	22	30000.00	Casper

Example: SELECT FROM Employees_Salary

WHERE Salary LIKE '4_ _ _ 0';

This SQL statement denotes that the Salary you want displayed in your resulting table are those that start with 4 and end with 0; all must be 5-digit numbers.

Using the base table, your resulting table would be:

Employees_Salary

Names	Age	Salary	City
Anderson, Ted	30	45000.00	Laramie
Dixon, Allan	27	43000.00	Chicago

Example: SELECT FROM Employees_Salary

WHERE Salary LIKE '%00';

The SQL query indicates that any value that ends with 00 will be displayed on the resulting table.

Employees_Salary

Names	Age	Salary	City
Williams, Michael	22	30000.00	Casper
Colton, Jean	24	37000.00	San Diego
Anderson, Ted	30	45000.00	Laramie
Dixon, Allan	27	43000.00	Chicago
Clarkson, Tim	25	35000.00	New York
Rogers, David	29	50000.00	San Francisco
Kennedy, Tom	27	34000.00	Denver

Since all the Salaries end with 00, they are all included in the output.

Example: SELECT FROM Employees_Salary

WHERE Salary LIKE '3_%_%_%_%';

The above SQL statement means that all values starting with 3 is followed by non-specified 4 more succeeding values. This will have to be a 5 digit-number displayed on the resulting table.

Employees_Salary

Names	Age	Salary	City
Williams, Michael	22	30000.00	Casper
Colton, Jean	24	37000.00	San Diego
Clarkson, Tim	25	35000.00	New York
Kennedy, Tom	27	34000.00	Denver

Example: SELECT FROM Employees_Salary

WHERE Salary LIKE '_00';

This SQL query is retrieving the values in the Salary column that have oo in the second and third positions.

Hence, the resulting table will be this:

Employees_Salary

Names	Age	Salary	City
Williams, Michael	22	30000.00	Casper
Rogers, David	29	50000.00	San Francisco

Example: SELECT FROM Employees_Salary

   WHERE Salary LIKE '_3%0';

This means that you want your output table to display values that have 3 in the second position and 0 at the end.

This will result to the table below:

Employees_Salary

Names	Age	Salary	City
Dixon, Allan	27	43000.00	Chicago

Isn't it amazing that you can modify the number data in your columns so easily with the use of SQL?

You can practice more to retain the information fully in your mind.

Chapter 32: Using ALIASES

Sometimes you need to rename a table to facilitate your SQL query. This renamed table are termed ALIASES.

They are only temporary and do not change the name of your base table in your databases.

ALIASES are useful when your SQL query uses more than one table; when you want to combine columns; when your column_names are long or vague and you want to change them for something simpler and clearer.

You can also use ALIASES when you want to define the functions in your SQL statement.

Here is an example of a SQL query using ALIASES:

For tables:

Example: SELECT "column_name1, "column_name2"

FROM "table_name" AS "alias_name"

WHERE [condition];

For columns:

Example: SELECT "column_name" AS "alias_name"

FROM "table_name"

WHERE [condition];

If these are your tables:

Table A

EnrolledStudents

IDNo	LastName	FirstName	Age
00100	Slater	Christian	21
00200	Lannister	Kerry	20
00300	Hall	Lenny	22
00400	Daniels	Willy	20
00500	Hanson	Gilbert	23

Table B

StudentsCourse

IDNo	Course	Year
00100	BSMT	1st
00200	BSBA	2nd year
00300	BSEd	1st year

00400	BSMT	3rd year
00500	BSPT	4th year

And you want to create an ALIAS for your columns, you can do it this way:

Example: SELECT LastName AS Last, FirstName AS first

FROM EnrolledStudents;

Your table output would be this:

EnrolledStudents

IDNo	Last	First	Age
00100	Slater	Christian	21
00200	Lannister	Kerry	20
00300	Hall	Lenny	22
00400	Daniels	Willy	20
00500	Hanson	Gilbert	23

Examples for ALIAS for tables:

The table EnrolledStudents will be represented with the small letter e, while the StudentsCourse will be represented with the small letter s.

Example: SELECT e.Last, e.First, s.course

FROM EnrolledStudents AS e, StudentsCourse AS s

WHERE s.course = BSMT AND e.IDNo = s.IDNo;

The resulting table will appear this way:

Last	First	Course
Slater	Christian	BSMT
Daniels	Willy	BSMT

You may add more conditions, depending on the table you would want to view or retrieve.

Chapter 33: Using the IN Operator

The IN operator is commonly used with the WHERE clause in a SQL query in specifying values.

The basic SQL syntax for the IN operator appears below.

Example: SELECT "column_name1", "column_name2,

...

FROM "table_name'

WHERE "column_name' IN (value1, value2,

value3, ...);

Sample table

OnlineStudents

Name	Age	Average	City	Country
Paterson, Diana	25	85	Chicago	USA
Cruz, Tom	21	91	Madrid	Spain
Walters, Ken	25	84	Vancouver	Canada
Leonard, Alex	23	87	New York	USA
White, John	20	78	Los Angeles	USA

Example: SELECT *

FROM OnlineStudents

WHERE Country IN ('USA', 'Spain');

This SQL statement will produce a table that appears this way:

Name	Age	Average	City	Country
Paterson, Diana	25	85	Chicago	USA
Cruz, Tom	21	91	Madrid	Spain
Leonard, Alex	23	87	New York	USA
White, John	20	78	Los Angeles	USA

As a beginner learning SQL, this is a significant operator for you because you will be using it often in creating basic SQLs.

Chapter 34: Using CLONE TABLES

CLONE TABLES are identical tables that you can create to perform particular SQL tasks.

These CLONE TABLES have exactly the same format and content with the original table, so you won't have problems practicing on them first.

Tables that are retrieved by using CREATE TABLE SELECT may not have the same indexes and other values as the original, so CLONE TABLES are best in this aspect.

You can do this by using the MySQL with the following steps:

1. **Retrieve the complete structure of your selected table.**

   Obtain a CREATE TABLE query by displaying the CREATE TABLE keywords.

2. **Rename the table and create another one.**

   Change the "table_name" to your CLONE TABLE name. After, you submit the query, you will have two identical tables.

3. **Execute step #2 and your CLONE TABLE is created.**

4. **To retain the data in the table, use the keyword INSERT INTO and SELECT.**

Purposes of CLONE TABLES

- To create sample tables that you can work on without being fearful you would destroy the whole table.

- To act as practice tables for beginners, so that the tables in the databases are safe and protected.

- To feature new interface for new users.

- To protect the integrity of the tables in your databases from new users.

CLONE TABLES can be very useful, if utilized properly. Know how to use them to your advantage.

Chapter 35: Using SQL EXPRESSIONS

SQL EXPRESSIONS make use of operators, characters, values and SQL functions that are combined to form a formula.

Numeric expressions

This expression is essential when forming SQL statements, where mathematical operations are needed.

The basic statement for this is:

> Example: SELECT expression AS operational_name
>
> FROM "table_name"
>
> WHERE condition;

Boolean Expressions

These are expressions that are used in matching single values.

The basic statement for this is:

> Example: SELECT "column_name1", "column_name2"
>
> FROM "table_name"
>
> WHERE SINGLE VALUE MATCHING EXPRESSION;

Sample table

> Sales

Name	TotalSales	ItemsSold	Date
Paterson, Diana	100.00	10	2/20/2016
Cruz, Tom	350.00	35	1/10/2016
Leonard, Alex	230.00	23	3/4/2016
White, John	420.00	42	4/26/2016
Brown, Dave	390.00	39	5/4/2016

If you want to extract the date of the TotalSales that is equivalent to 100, you can use this SQL statement:

Example: SELECT *

FROM Sales

WHERE TotalSales = 100;

Your resulting table would look like this:

Sales

Name	TotalSales	ItemsSold	Date
Paterson, Diana	100.00	10	2/20/2016

Date expressions

Date expressions are used for dates, understandably. They help extract the time values, and sometimes the current system date.

The basic SQL may appear like this:

Example: SELECT GETDATE ();

These are the SQL expressions that you can use according to the data you want to retrieve.

Chapter 36: Using VIEWS in SQL

VIEWS are virtual tables or stored SQL queries in the databases that have predefined queries and unique names. They are actually the resulting tables from your SQL queries.

As a beginner, you may want to learn about how you can use VIEWS. Among their numerous uses is their flexibility can combine rows and columns from VIEWS.

Here are important pointers and advantages in using VIEWS:

1. You can summarize data from different tables, or a subset of columns from various tables.

2. You can control what users of your databases can see, and restrict what you don't want them to view.

3. You can organize your database for your users' easy manipulation, while simultaneously protecting your non-public files.

4. You can modify, or edit, or UPDATE your data. Sometimes there are limitations, though, such as, being able to access only one column when using VIEW.

5. You can create columns from various tables for your reports.

6. You can increase the security of your databases because VIEWS can display only the information that you want displayed. You can protect specific information from other users.

7. You can provide easy and efficient accessibility or access paths to your data to users.

8. You can allow users of your databases to derive various tables from your data without dealing with the complexity of your databases.

9. You can rename columns through views. If you are a website owner, VIEWS can also provide domain support.

10. The WHERE clause in the SQL VIEWS query may not contain subqueries.

11. For the INSERT keyword to function, you must include all NOT NULL columns from the original table.

12. Do not use the WITH ENCRIPTION (unless utterly necessary) clause for your VIEWS because you may not be able to retrieve the SQL.

13. Avoid creating VIEWS for each base table (original table). This can add more workload in managing your databases. As long as you create your base SQL query properly, there is no need to create VIEWS for each base table.

14. VIEWS that use the DISTINCT and ORDER BY clauses or keywords may not produce the expected results.

15. VIEWS can be updated under the condition that the SELECT clause may not contain the summary functions; and/or the set operators, and the set functions.

16. When UPDATING, there should be a synchronization of your base table with your VIEWS table. Therefore, you must analyze the VIEW table, so that the data presented are still correct, each time you UPDATE the base table.

17. Avoid creating VIEWS that are unnecessary because this will clutter your catalogue.

18. Specify "column_names" clearly.

19. The FROM clause of the SQL VIEWS query may not contain many tables, unless specified.

20. The SQL VIEWS query may not contain HAVING or GROUP BY.

21. The SELECT keyword can join your VIEW table with your base table.

How to create VIEWS

You can create VIEWS through the following easy steps:

Step #1 - Check if your system is appropriate to implement VIEW queries.

Step #2 - Make use of the CREATE VIEW SQL statement.

Step #3 – Use key words for your SQL syntax just like with any other SQL main queries.

Step #4 – Your basic CREATE VIEW statement or syntax will appear like this:

Example: Create view view_"table_name AS

SELECT "column_name1"

FROM "table_name"

WHERE [condition];

Let's have a specific example based on our original table.

EmployeesSalary

175

Names	Age	Salary	City
Williams, Michael	22	30000.00	Casper
Colton, Jean	24	37000.00	San Diego
Anderson, Ted	30	45000.00	Laramie
Dixon, Allan	27	43000.00	Chicago
Clarkson, Tim	25	35000.00	New York
Alaina, Ann	32	41000.00	Ottawa
Rogers, David	29	50000.00	San Francisco
Lambert, Jancy	38	47000.00	Los Angeles
Kennedy, Tom	27	34000.00	Denver
Schultz, Diana	40	46000.00	New York

Based on the table above, you may want to create a view of the customers' name and the City only. This is how you should write your statement.

Example: CREATE VIEW EmployeesSalary_VIEW AS

SELECT Names, City

FROM EmployeesSalary;

From the resulting VIEW table, you can now create a query such as the statement below.

SELECT * FROM EmployeesSalary_VIEW;

This SQL query will display a table that will appear this way:

EmployeesSalary

Names	City
Williams, Michael	Casper
Colton, Jean	San Diego
Anderson, Ted	Laramie
Dixon, Allan	Chicago
Clarkson, Tim	New York
Alaina, Ann	Ottawa
Rogers, David	San Francisco
Lambert, Jancy	Los Angeles
Kennedy, Tom	Denver
Schultz, Diana	New York

Using the keyword WITH CHECK OPTION

These keywords ascertain that there will be no return errors with the INSERT and UPDATE returns, and that all conditions are fulfilled properly.

> Example: CREATE VIEW "table_Name"_VIEW AS
>
> SELECT "column_name1", "column_name2"
>
> FROM "table_name"
>
> WHERE [condition]
>
> WITH CHECK OPTION;

Applying this SQL statement to the same conditions (display name and city), we can come up now with our WITH CHECK OPTION statement.

> Example: CREATE VIEW EmployeesSalary_VIEW AS
>
> SELECT Names, City
>
> FROM EmployeesSalary
>
> WHERE City IS NOT NULL
>
> WITH CHECK OPTION;

The SQL query above will ensure that there will be no NULL returns in your resulting table.

DROPPING VIEWS

You can drop your VIEWS whenever you don't need them anymore. The SQL syntax is the same as the main SQL statements.

Example: DROP VIEW EmployeesSalary_VIEW;

UPDATING VIEWS

You can easily UPDATE VIEWS by following the SQL query for main queries.

Example: CREATE OR REPLACE VIEW "tablename"_VIEWS (could also be VIEWS_'tablename") AS

SELECT "column_name"

FROM "table_name"

WHERE condition;

DELETING VIEWS

The SQL syntax for DELETING VIEWS is much the same way as DELETING DATA using the main SQL query. The difference only is in the name of the table.

If you use the VIEW table example above, and want to delete the City column, you can come up with this SQL statement.

Example: DELETE FROM EmployeesSalary_VIEW

179

WHERE City = 'New York';

The SQL statement above would have this output:

EmployeesSalary

Names	Age	Salary	City
Williams, Michael	22	30000.00	Casper
Colton, Jean	24	37000.00	San Diego
Anderson, Ted	30	45000.00	Laramie
Dixon, Allan	27	43000.00	Chicago
Alaina, Ann	32	41000.00	Ottawa
Rogers, David	29	50000.00	San Francisco
Lambert, Jancy	38	47000.00	Los Angeles
Kennedy, Tom	27	34000.00	Denver

INSERTING ROWS

Creating an SQL in INSERTING ROWS is similar to the UPDATING VIEWS syntax. Make sure you have included the NOT NULL columns.

Example: INSERT INTO "table_name"_VIEWS "column_name1"

WHERE value1;

VIEWS can be utterly useful, if you utilize them appropriately.

Chapter 37: SQL and Subqueries

In SQL, subqueries are queries within queries. The subqueries usually use the WHERE clause. Also called nested query or internal query, subqueries can also restrict the data being retrieved.

Creating subqueries are more complex than creating simple queries. You have to use essential key words such as, SELECT, DELETE, UPDATE, INSERT and the operators such as, BETWEEN (used only WITHIN a subquery and not WITH a subquery), IN, =, < =, > =, >, <, < >, and similar symbols.

In the previous chapters we have used subqueries a lot of times with the key word WHERE.

In this chapter, we would learn more about this vital keyword that is considered by many database programmers as the heart of SQL.

In composing a subquery, you have to remember these pointers.

1. It must be enclosed with an open and close parentheses.

2. It can be used in several ways.

3. It is recommended that a subquery can run on its own.

4. It can ascribe column values for files.

5. It can be found anywhere in the main query. You can identify it because it is enclosed in parentheses.

6. If it displays more than one row in response to an SQL command, this can only be accepted when there are multiple value operators. Example is the IN operator.

7. In a subquery, the GROUP BY is used instead of the ORDER BY, which is used in the main statement or query.

8. When creating subqueries, do not enclose it immediately in a set function.

9. To create subqueries, it is easier to start with a FROM statement.

10. Subqueries should also have names for easy identification.

11. When using the SELECT key word, only one column should be included in your subquery. The exception is when the main query has selected many columns for comparison.

12. Values that refer to a National Character Large Object (NCLOB), Binary Large Object (BLOB), Character Large Object (CLOB) and an Array, which is part of a collection data in variable sizes, should NOT be included in your SELECT list.

There are several examples already from the previous chapters, but here are more:

Example #1 – Subqueries with SELECT key word or statement

SELECT "column_name1" FROM "table_name1"

WHERE value IN (SELECT "column_name2" FROM "table_name2' WHERE condition);

The above SQL query and subquery could also be written this way:

SELECT "column_name1"

FROM "table_name1"

WHERE value IN

(SELECT "column_name2"

FROM "table_name2 WHERE condition);

Let's apply the SQL statement in the two tables below:

Address

Street	City	State
67 7th St.	Los Angeles	California
10 18th St.	Casper	Wyoming
1020 Quincy Ave.	Chicago	Illinois
1019 Reed Ave.	Cheyenne	Wyoming
23 18th St.	San Diego	California

Online_Employees

Name	State	Age
Sarah Hawkins	Colorado	56
Noel Stevens	Florida	55

Lena Dawson	Minnesota	26
Timothy Pearson	Alaska	29
Allen Bailey	Wyoming	43

Your SQL query or statement would appear like this:

Example: SELECT State

FROM Address

WHERE City IN

(SELECT State

FROM Online_Employees

WHERE Age = > 60);

The above SQL query can be expressed without indentation, but programmers prefer to indent because this identifies more easily the subqueries or inner and outer queries.

SELECT State FROM Address WHERE City IN

(SELECT Age FROM Online_Employees

WHERE Age = > 60);

Use your subqueries properly to extract the data you need. You can review the subqueries that were discussed in the previous chapters.

Chapter 38: How SQL Injections Can Destroy Databases

Your databases can be destroyed easily by malicious persons with SQL injections. These thoughtless hackers can insert a code into your SQL statements through the web and damage your databases.

Hence, if you have plans of creating your own website, you must be aware of this so that you can avoid or prevent it from happening. The most common method is to hack into passwords and user names or IDs.

Hackers usually insert a number or a symbol that can change the returns of your SQL query.

Here's how you can minimize this incident from happening.

1. Create a BLACKLIST of words that are not allowed in the SQL statements submitted. If you are a website administrator, you will be screening out and minimizing the hacking of your website.

   This is not a full proof protection though, because most of the characters and symbols in SQL statements or queries are commonly used.

2. Utilize SQL PARAMETERS after your SQL query has been submitted. The symbol of PARAMETERS is @ .

   Example #1: SELECT * FROM Visitors WHERE VisitorId = @0";

Example #2: INSERT INTO Students (StudentName, Age, City) Values (@1, @2, @3);

In the examples above, a malicious code (number) could not be inserted because the parameters have limited any addition of a new number.

3. Double check your SQL queries or syntax, so that this cannot be easily tampered with.

4. If you are a database user, submit your queries to websites that are proven legitimate.

5. If you are unsure of your SQL syntax, don't input it or be nonchalant about it. When uncertain, don't use it.

Although, not all SQL users will be concerned with hacking, it pays to know these basic prevention skills and be on the lookout for these malicious codes.

Chapter 39: Additional Pointers in Using SQL

There are significant pointers that you must know as a SQL beginner. Take note of them and enrich your SQL learning process.

1. **Be aware that there may be other versions of the SQL queries**. SQL has been extraordinarily helpful in modifying tables that many developers had created SQL syntax for their own applications. So, be open to new SQL statements.

2. **Ensure that your computer is durable, if you plan to establish your own database**. A computer that is not protected from viruses may have all of its databases corrupted.

3. **Be patient in learning.** There are no shortcuts to success; you have to go through the ups and downs.

4. **Persistence is the key**. No matter how hard the task is, if you are persistent and you persevere, you will never fail. As the cliche goes: A quitter never wins, and a winner NEVER quits."

5. **Be positive.** An optimistic attitude will help you learn more quickly. This is because you are motivated in searching for the positive things that await you.

6. **Learn one chapter at a time.** No one is keeping tab of the time, so take your time. Munch the information slowly until your mind has digested the information sufficiently.

7. **Learn the limitations of your DBMS (database management system).** It is only in knowing this that you can modify your tables effectively.

8. **Avoid taxing your SQL server by creating unnecessary queries.** If you don't need all the columns, refrain from using * and select only the columns that you need. Submitting useless queries will only slow down your system.

9. **There are certain SQL statements that can be easier to use in fetching tables**. Remember the queries and apply whichever is more preferable for you.

10. **Ascertain that your 'table_names" are unique and have a fully qualified name**. You would not want retrieving two tables when all you needed is one. It is time consuming. Time is gold.

11. **Practice makes perfect; t**herefore, do not be afraid to practice on some SQL databases or tables.

12. **Invite a friend to learn SQL with you.** Many beginners prefer to learn with someone. This is due to the fact that they can challenge and motivate each other. But, of course, if you prefer learning alone, then that would not be a problem.

13. **Keep a logbook of your learning activities**. Through this method, you can monitor your progress and assess your knowledge.

14. **Apply what you have learned.** Learning can only be verified when you are able to apply it, so don't be afraid to create and tweak your own databases.

15. **Share your knowledge with others**. As you share it, you are also mastering and retaining the information more effectively.

These are simple tips that can help you optimize your SQL learning process. Apply them and be a master SQL expert eventually.

Chapter 40: SQL Quiz

Okay, so are you ready now to test how much you have learned about basic SQL?

Here are 10 questions to test your basic knowledge about SQL syntax or queries.

All SQL statements should be based on this table:

EmployeesSalary

Names	Age	Salary	City
Williams Michael	22	30000.00	Casper
Colton Jean	24	37000.00	San Diego
Anderson Ted	30	45000.00	Laramie
Dixon Allan	27	43000.00	Chicago
Clarkson Tim	25	35000.00	New York
Alaina Ann	32	41000.00	Ottawa
Rogers David	29	50000.00	San Francisco
Lambert Jancy	38	47000.00	Los Angeles
Kennedy Tom	27	34000.00	Denver
Schultz Diana	40	46000.00	New York

Answer the questions first before looking at the correct answers. Here goes:

1. Transcribe SQL.

2. What is the keyword in creating tables?

3. What is the SQL syntax in selecting tables?

4. What is the keyword in deleting tables?

5. What is the SQL statement if you want to display only the names and the city of the table above?

6. What is the SQL statement if you want to retrieve only the data of employees who are 25 years old and above?

7. What is the SQL command if you want to arrange the names in an ascending order?

8. What is the SQL query if you want to fetch the data of employees, who have a salary of more than 20000.00?

9. What is the SQL command if you want to select only the employees coming from Denver?

10. What is the SQL if you want to change the Name of Lambert Jancy to Walker Jean?

Easy? Oh yes! You should know the answers, as a beginner.

Try to answer all of them first, before checking on the correct answers.

Now, let's check if you have the correct answers.

ANSWERS:

1. STRUCTURED QUERY LANGUAGE

2. CREATE TABLE

3. SELECT "column_name1", "column_name2 FROM "table_name";

   (Remember to remove the double quotes when substituting the names of your columns and tables.)

4. DELETE TABLE

5. SELECT Names, City FROM EmployeesSalary;

6. SELECT * FROM EmployeesSalary
   WHERE Age >= 25;

7. SELECT * FROM EmployeesSalary
   ORDER BY Names ASC;

8. SELECT * FROM EmployeesSalary
   WHERE Salary >20000;

9. SELECT * FROM EmployeesSalary

WHERE City = 'Denver';

10. UPDATE EmployeesSalary

    SET Names = 'Walker Jean'

    WHERE Names = 'Lambert Jancy';

So, how many correct answers did you get?

They are easy questions. I hope you got a perfect score. If not, then no sweat! Just review the chapters again and repeat the quiz.

Take note that the keywords such as, UPDATE, goes hand in hand with SET and WHERE.

UPDATE, SET WHERE. This is only one item, so create your own 'MEMORY NOTES'.

Conclusion

Learning the SQL language can be laborious and tedious, but if you have genuine interest in learning a new language and updating your skills, it could be relatively easy.

In this book, all the basic information that you need to learn as a beginner are presented. All you have to do is to apply them.

Now that you have read the book, you can go back for the details that you may forget along the way.

If you have properly studied the contents of this book, you could construct your basic SQL syntax easily.

Challenge

Now, here is your challenge. Create your own database in your computer and organize your tables systematically for future retrieval.

If at first, you do not succeed, don't give up. It took more than 80 years to build the pyramids of Egypt. However, the impossible was done, anyhow. At present, they are still phenomenal structures that make people stare in awe.

Go, build your own database and watch it slowly grow into a reliable and organized information base. For sure, you would learn to value your databases as the stored data multiply by leaps and bounds.

Good luck with your databases, and do not be afraid to accept the challenge!

Thank you again for buying this book!

Finally, if you enjoyed this book, then I'd like to ask you for a favor, would you be kind enough to leave a review for this book on Amazon? It'd be greatly appreciated!

Made in the USA
Lexington, KY
28 February 2018